Buzz About This Book

This is a must read for any woman who wants to learn practical and actionable tips to break through any barrier and advance in leadership. Men would also be wise to learn from these tips and to imitate the innate skills women have if they want to increase their competitive edge and effectiveness. For all who want to succeed, this book, if read and applied, will help you become a more impactful servant-leader!

Jerry Amante ~ Senior Vice President & General Counsel, Core Strategic Group and Mayor, City of Tustin (Retired)

~~~~

I have always thought that leadership in its simplest definition is about influence. Lacy Schoen has written a terrific book about influence that focuses on five key strengths that women (and frankly men as well) should focus on for the greatest impact. It's an easy to read book with easy to implement strategies that can have a powerful impact on women's careers.

Mike Groff ~ President/CEO (Retired) Toyota and Lexus Financial Services.

~~~~

Using the five innate female strengths as a guide, Lacy Schoen has given every businesswoman the secret to their own success. It took her skill to show us these "secrets" were hiding in plain sight; we just needed them presented in a concise, readable package. With personal insight, Lacy clearly shows the hallmarks of what it takes to make it in a culture that requires a fine tuned set of tools. This book is the blue print to move your career to the next level.

Julienne Chené ~ Author, Food for Talk and Senior Producer, California Insider

Whether you are a couple of years into your career, mid-level, or even seasoned, Schoen's book is a great read with lots of gems. Schoen shares inspirational stories that illustrate the 5 innate qualities that women (and men) already possess. Then she gives concrete examples of each concept along with specific steps toward leveraging each quality. Schoen's book will lift both your spirits and your career!

Cynthia K. West, Ph.D. ~ Author of Techno-Human Mesh, VP of Global Sales for Drop Kitchen

~~~~

I loved this book; I only wish someone would have handed it to me at the onset of my career. The concepts that Lacy shares are simple because they are rooted in human truth. I especially liked the chapter on Giving and how this simple shift in approach begins the process of receiving. A must read for working women who want to set themselves on a course for both success and fulfillment.

Klara Farkas ~ Director, Executive Career Development, Executive MBA Programs, UCI Paul Merage School of Business

~~~~

"Advancing Through Influence" is a valuable book for anyone who wants to learn how to advance their career using skills and strengths they already have. In this book, Lacy Schoen identifies 5 innate female strengths and describes how we can use these strengths to get to where we want to go. Through examples, practical tips, and personal stories, Lacy shows how we can each tap our inner resources, advance in our careers and make our unique mark in the world.

Goli Sadri, Ph.D. ~ California State University, Fullerton, Professor of Management & Director, Women's Leadership Program

Imagine if you held in your hands a roadmap that shows you step-by-step strategies on how to advance faster in your profession, while building skills that come naturally to you. With her signature straight talk and humor, Lacy Schoen expertly guides you in her must-read book for any woman serious about moving forward in her career and life. I wish I had this book after graduating from business school. I plan to give extra copies of this book as gifts to my female friends and also a few men I know who'd appreciate Lacy's insights and wisdom.

Fairbourne Frye ~ MBA, CEO and Founder, Insight Catalyst

~~~~

As a believer in the change acceleration process and stakeholder management, I was able to draw analogies between those business approaches and the guidance in this book to my personal success. As a prior CEO for ten years, I wish this book had been available back then for my personal use and sharing with other executives. The insights regarding five innate strengths, including case studies, are actionable, practical, and measurable for ongoing self-improvement, reflection and mentoring of others. The author's conversational approach made this a quick read, feeling at times as though she and I were chatting over a cup of coffee and brainstorming.

Caryn Siebert ~ Insurance Executive (C Suite), Independent Director and Philanthropist

~~~~

Whether you are just starting out in your career or have become a seasoned leader, this is a must-read book for all female professionals facing barriers or obstacles to success. Through Lacy's personal stories and experience overcoming power structures, you will be empowered with practical tools you can use right away to give you the confidence and courage you need to thrive as a female leader in the workplace. Lacy's authentic and warm-hearted writing style will give you the sense that you have a personal friend and coach cheering you on through each chapter of her book.

Nicole Suydam ~ President & CEO, Goodwill of Orange County

~~~~

"Advancing through Influence" is hands-down the most action-able book on leadership that I've read. It stands out because it is written specifically for women laying out strategies to au-thentically advance our careers through influence. Lacy breaks down how men gain influence with each other and points to five female strengths that we can leverage to obtain access to circles of power. The book is potent, yet succinct and practical —a game-changer for powerful women set on breaking through the glass ceiling.

Stefanie Robel, Ph.D. ~ Neuroscientist, Professor Virginia Tech Fralin Biomedical Research Institute, President/ CEO, Team Leadership in Research

~~~~

Women have been told to act like men if they want to succeed in business and to get where they want to go in their careers. This book teaches us that we can remain who we are, and use our own innate strengths of emoting, relationship-building, and giving to achieve success just as much. In her book, Lacy demonstrates how we can use our emotions safely, the right and healthy way to elicit response from influencers, and clear steps on how to find and use our voice.

Katerina Hencova ~ Financial Planner, Continuum Consulting Group

ADVANCING THROUGH
INFLUENCE

*Using Your 5 Innate Female Strengths to Break Through
Power Barriers and Advance Your Career*

Lacy Schoen

Powerful You!
PUBLISHING
Sharing Wisdom ~ Shining Light

Advancing Through Influence
Using Your 5 Innate Female Strengths to Break Through Power Barriers and Advance Your Career

Copyright © 2021

Published by: Powerful You! Inc. USA
powerfulyoupublishing.com

Library of Congress Control Number: 2021909905

Lacy Schoen—First Edition

ISBN: 978-1-7356579-4-3

First Edition July 2021

BUSINESS & ECONOMICS / Women in Business

Dedication

First, this book is dedicated to my daughter, Tenaya, who not only wields massive female influence but has also broken through countless barriers to lead and find her voice. You are the total package: bold yet gentle, fierce but wise. People are drawn to you. I'm so proud to be your mom, and of the wonderful example you are for your own daughter. #breakthecycle

I would also like to dedicate this book to the women who want to advance in their careers but feel they have run into a power structure or workplace barrier that is preventing or slowing their advancement. You are the reason I do this work—to help you leverage your female strengths, advance in your career, and change the world with your leadership.

Acknowledgments

I want to thank my daughter, Tenaya. There's no other woman I'm closer with. Your unconditional love, admiration, and encouragement is foundational in my life. Thank you for the conversations we've had and continue to have on the topic of women's empowerment.

I want to thank my husband, Dean, for his consistent and undying love, respect, and support. I am especially grateful for your openness to have difficult conversations about the subtle behavioral habits between men and women that often fly under the radar, yet drag women down.

I want to thank my dear friend Jerry Amante who, although a man, has all the female strengths discussed in this book. Thank you for being a mentor, business partner, and friend that has been willing to go to bat for me over and over again, even when it involved risk. You know I learned so much from you.

I also want to thank my friend Dr. Goli Sadri. It is because of your encouragement that this book finally got written. Thank you for pushing me. And thank you for giving me such a meaningful role in helping the next generation of women leaders kick off their careers by breaking through barriers from the start.

I want to thank Mike Groff and Caryn Seibert for taking the time to help me refine the content of this book so that it can more effectively fulfill its mission to help women advance.

Lastly, I want to thank the people in my career who have tried to limit my progress, who have thrown marbles in my path, or tried to minimize my contributions. I would like to thank everyone who has ever told me I can't. You have given me such a valuable gift, and that is to believe in myself and to figure out a way. Through you, I've learned fortitude, perseverance, and the profoundly powerful strengths I possess as a woman. You've taught me that I can achieve anything I want to achieve, and that I can do it with integrity in spite of negative circumstances. And thank you for inspiring this book, so that other women can also learn to leverage their strengths to overcome barriers and gain the success they crave, regardless of the people that needlessly stand in their way.

Table of Contents

"The most common way people give up their power is by thinking they don't have any."
Alice Walker

Introduction

Hi friend! Welcome to *Advancing Through Influence: Using Your 5 Innate Female Strengths to Break Through Power Barriers and Advance Your Career.*

My name is Lacy Schoen, and I'm the founder of Real Women Real Success, a woman's coach and a consultant for the Women's Leadership Program at the Cal State Fullerton's College of Business and Economics. I also have a jewelry company, a real estate investment firm, and a training company called Team Lead, Inc.; and last but not least, I serve on the Board of the Childhood Drowning Prevention Foundation. Prior to all I'm doing now, I had a thirty-year career in nonprofit management—twenty of them as a CEO—and was mostly involved in various segments of government and public policy. In my last CEO position, I founded, built from the ground up, and ran a nonprofit focused on collaborative public policy.

It was in this last nonprofit job that my ability to Advance Through Influence using my own female strengths was fully revealed to me. I realized, perhaps for the first time, just how powerful we, as women, can be.

The year was 2010, and I was running a nonprofit, the members of which were cities and one hundred seventy-six of their elected officials. We were a chapter of a larger nonprofit with which my members and board of directors had strong, foundational disagreements. Over the course of the previous year the board had made a number of attempts to compromise with our parent organization, to no avail. We were an organization in crisis, and I was facing the most challenging dilemma of my career.

Eventually, the board decided to close our chapter and start a new, independent nonprofit; however, they would only do this if I agreed to be its CEO. Given the current situation, I was open to the idea. Our members were leaving left and right and taking their checkbooks with them.

The CEO of the parent organization made his position very clear. He said, "If your members drop their dues and there's not enough money to pay you and your staff, you'll all be out of a job." It wasn't what I wanted to hear, but I appreciated his frankness. It let me know what I needed to do.

I found that I wasn't just acting out of fear of the old organization failing, but excitement about heading up a new, more collaborative one, where I would be able to carry out my commitment to servant leadership with more integrity. Also integral to my decision was the commitment, made by several of my board members and a few additional elected officials, to leverage their influence to make the new organization a reality.

There were significant hurdles to overcome, like money, time, and nasty politics. The core team of elected officials—about nine people I'll refer to as the "dream team"—worked tirelessly to deal with all of this and getting the votes needed to launch the new nonprofit.

One of the biggest challenges was the glacial pace of government decision-making. At the local level, all decisions—for example, whether to join a new organization—were made at the biweekly city council meetings. (Imagine, in business, only being able to make decisions every two weeks!) What's more, these city council meetings are where the decision to join the new organization had to happen. Along with this limitation was the fact that it took time—sometimes weeks—just to get on a city council agenda. Once this happened, my dream team then needed to convince three of the five members of each city council to vote "yes" to join the new organization.

In order to make it work financially and be able to pay our staff, we needed two-thirds of our thirty-four cities to commit. We were also under a time constraint. It was the end of September when the board voted to ramp down the old nonprofit and create the new one, so the dream team had just twelve short weeks to make it happen. You see, we were on a calendar year budget. We invoiced for dues late in December and that money carried us through the following year. This time, with the closing of the chapter doors, no new invoices would be going out unless they were for the new nonprofit. We would literally run out of money on December 31.

As if this wasn't enough, we were in an election year during the Great Recession. A predominant political strategy was attacking one's opponent with accusations of reckless spending—like voting to join a new organization that didn't yet exist.

My influential dream team was working hard, but six weeks in we only had one third of the cities needed. Things were not going as planned. Cities were taking too long to vote and now neither the old nor the new organization had enough money to maintain our staff. The baby had been split.

We felt we were making real headway when a member of the dream team influencers met with a few City Managers to get their support for placing the vote on the new organization on their respective council meeting agendas. Unfortunately, this strategy proved to be a failure. Not only were the City Managers angry about the request and how it was made, some of them actively started working against the cause!

Then, the first week of November, ultimate disaster struck when all but four of the dream team lost their re-election campaigns! My heart sank that night as I slumped in my bed, glass of wine in hand, watching the poll results on my laptop. I knew that the remaining dream team members had already done what they could to advance the cause. The fight, it would seem, was over.

Tears of fear and sadness welled up in me. I cared about these people, and I believed in our revolution, so much so that I had gladly bet my job and career on it. Sure, I knew there was a risk, but I never anticipated this disaster. Neither had the dream team, apparently; they had spent so much time on the new organization that they had paid no attention to their own campaigns. Now, with the loss of these influencers, I was facing the very real possibility of losing my job. Thoughts of losing my home and not being able to put my kids through college raced through my mind. I also feared having a black mark on my name. As noble as my motivation was, I felt it would be hard to articulate in a job interview.

Somehow, out of my fear grew personal resolve. Maybe it was bravery, or maybe it was having no other option. I bounced back quickly, and when I woke up the next morning, I decided, "I am going to make this happen. Failure is not an option."

I had only six weeks left to get double the number of commitments the dream team had already secured. To do it, I would have to utilize every asset in my toolbox. And I did just that. I went to council meetings. I gave presentations. I leveraged my relationships with the remnants of the dream team. I met with people. I made deals. I helped elected officials get positions they wanted. I did a lot of selling. I did a lot of promising. I did a lot of tapdancing. I found every way I could to compel these cities, City Managers, and their elected leaders to get on board. I worked day and night.

When I woke up the morning of December 20, I saw I had a text message. It said "Lacy, we met in closed session last night. Lake Forest is in!" That was our twenty-first city, and got us what we needed to just barely cover our staff costs and start the new organization. With just nine days of funding left, I had obtained the commitments needed to launch the new organization.

I would lead that organization for the next five years. During that time I was able to triple it in size and accomplish more than we had ever envisioned. What I learned about myself through those events will serve me for the rest of my life.

Shortly after leaving the organization to work on my new passion—supporting women—I was asked to co-author a book with nineteen other female authors called *Keys to Conscious Business Growth*. When I asked what I should write about, the publishers replied, "Why don't you share the biggest career challenge you've ever faced and how you overcame it?"

I really had to think about this—not about what the biggest challenge was (it was clearly what I just shared with you)—but how I had overcome it. I had never given that much thought before. Now, for the first time, I asked myself, "How the heck DID I do that?" I thought about it for two weeks before writing a word, and at the end of that two weeks I realized two things:

1.   Every strategy I used to overcome that crisis was

a strength that came naturally to me as a woman; and

2. Every success over the course of my entire career was the result of leaning on these strengths.
Every time I was not so successful I had failed to
employ these strengths.

It was at that point that I really solidified, and put names to,
the five innate female strengths that I had been (unknowing-
ly) leveraging for decades. I realized as women we innately
have within us everything we need to win. All we have to do
is become MORE of who we already are, and apply those
strengths wisely and strategically.

Why is this so important? Women make up 51% of the population, 50% of the workforce, and 57% of college graduates,
yet we are only 8% of Fortune 500 CEOs. We make up only
34% of government executives, and we get less than 3% of
venture capital investments. Think about this: within the last
few years there have been more Fortune 500 CEOs named
John than there were women CEOs. Talk about insulting!

Women are overrepresented in support roles, and under-
represented in executive roles. The higher the role, the more
the percentage of women decreases. And when it comes to
elected office here in the United States, women hold between
24% and 30%, depending on the level of government. While
women do seem to be making inroads with regard to government jobs, they are still way behind in private industry, both
nationally and worldwide.

Even more disheartening, as of the writing of this book,
women have fallen 8% in the pay gap since 2015, making

only 82 cents for every dollar men made in 2020. The global pandemic hit women hardest, with their numbers in the labor force dropping to a thirty-three-year low, as women took on a disproportionate load of care-giving and remote schooling demands.

These statistics propelled me to become an advocate of women, encouraging them to take matters into their own hands, breaking through barriers, and influencing their way to the top. That's the mission of this book and my coaching practice.

Why does it matter that women are behind? It's not just because women have proven time and time again to be as competent as men (whether or not they are perceived as such); or that profits increase when women are equally represented at the top; or that, as Tony Robbins shares in his well-researched book, *Money, Mastering the Game*, women tend to be more pragmatic and successful investors than men, because men are overconfident. It's because when we take a critical look at the problem-solving strategies taken by our communities, businesses, and governments, it's often the female strengths that are missing. Indeed, study after study has shown that having more women at the top creates more balanced solutions, more creative problem-solving, and more sensitivity in the work environment. Yes, there are many great men that wield these strengths with equal finesse, but why wouldn't we utilize the people for whom those strengths come naturally? We need women in leadership positions to help solve the world's most complex problems. I don't advocate for any woman, but honest, service-minded women who are collaborative and desire to bring people together rather than serve a personal agenda. The women I coach and teach have honest intentions and belong in leadership.

So why are we not at the top, ladies? I must warn you, you may not like my answer, but it is an honest one, based not only on my experience but those of the women I teach, coach, and talk to. Oftentimes, women don't help each other to succeed in a work setting. Over the course of my career I found support from other women to be fairly dismal; in fact, I had more women try to undercut me than help me while men were my biggest supporters and sponsors. Now, I know that this isn't true everywhere, but judging from my stories and those I've heard over the years, it is all too common.

Have you ever heard "There's nothing more powerful than a woman with a tribe?" Well, that's what we need—"professional female friends communities" made up of women helping each other succeed. This is not just about lending emotional support, but about *sponsorship*—taking some sort of action on behalf of another woman that helps her advance or reach her goal—be it making an introduction, advocating for her to get a job, or introducing her to an influencer that can help her—just like good old boys clubs have always done for men. It means using our influence to give other good and honest women a leg up. I want to be a force for that, and this book (along with my coaching and consulting) is my way of supporting you as a member of your female friends community. It's my way of investing what I know to help more women, including you, get where they want and need to be.

I say it's time for another revolution. It's time for women to step up and leverage our strengths to claim our positions in leadership. To do this, we must stop waiting for our organizations' leadership to change or get a clue about our value. I believe women are ready and WANT to take matters into their own hands. And I want you to know exactly how to do that. You CAN do it. You can influence your own success on your time, rather than the timetables of others.

In reading this book, you are taking the first step. My advice is that you really take the words in it to heart. Learn about, practice, hone and leverage your five innate female strengths to build your influence, break through power barriers and advance your career. In doing so, you will not only create your own path to success, you will make a positive impact on a world that needs and is waiting for your leadership!

Setting Yourself Up for Success

First, I want to take a minute to applaud you for taking the initiative to improve your understanding of your own innate female strengths, and for committing to advancing yourself. This is important to me personally, because you are needed in the world, at a higher level of leadership, and I'm going to help you get there. Before we begin, I'm going to share some best practices, success factors, caveats and general wisdom that will help you gain the most from this book.

I encourage you to read the entire book before you immerse yourself in a full effort to leverage your strengths. The reason is that they often work in concert. Think of them like an orchestra; sometimes, one strength will play louder than the others, but then they come together all working in harmony. When you get the hang of it, they become an invaluable toolbox that you can artfully and spontaneously access in any situation.

Here are some additional things I want you to know.

I'm going to be making some generalizations. Some might even call them stereotypes. What I am endeavoring to do is to address the situations that are most common in the workforce. Yes, there are always exceptions, but that is not our focus here. Instead, we will address what most often occurs and thus rely on these generalizations, even if they are not true one hundred percent of the time.

I also want to be clear that I am not, and will never, suggest that you do anything inappropriate. This book, in large part, is about using your strengths to build influential relationships that are platonic and professional. If an interaction or relationship that you are building becomes uncomfortable, I encourage you to discontinue it right away. You don't need to do anything improper or unseemly to have influence or succeed.

Some of the strategies and behaviors I suggest may not come naturally to you right now, but they will with your commitment and effort. I'm not telling you to "fake" interest, gestures, or sentiment with anybody. What I am suggesting is that you cultivate within yourself a genuine interest in others. First, people know when someone is not being authentic; second, taking a genuine interest in others is the mark of a good leader and that's what you're here for—to grow your own leadership skills.

Occasionally, I'll talk about the differences between male and female approaches to certain situations, and teach you how to use your strengths to play the same game men are often playing. That said, I don't want you to get the idea that I do not like men or that men are the enemy. I love men. Men have always supported and promoted me. The truth of the matter is that to be truly successful all leaders need both male and female strengths. This was evident in the leadership styles of some of my favorite male leaders—for instance, Nelson Mandela or Martin Luther King Jr., who had as many female strengths in play as they did male strengths.

I also want to ask you to be responsible with the information I'm going to share with you. You are powerful beyond belief, and just like any power, yours can be misused in order to manipulate. I'm putting my faith in you that you are pursuing knowledge of self and your strengths to use for good. If you don't intend to use them for good and check in with your values regularly, then put this book down. It's not for you.

It is imperative that you read this book with an open mind. I find that sometimes adults, especially if they have had some successes under the belt, have barriers to learning new concepts. Here are the three thoughts that will keep you from learning something new:

1. I already knew that.
2. That doesn't apply to me.
3. I disagree.

Keeping an open mind means not saying these things to yourself. Instead, approach everything with a clean slate and figure out how you can apply what is being taught to your specific situation.

As mentioned, this book is about learning how to grow your influence. It is therefore important to understand that there are two types of influence: Borrowed Influence and Earned Influence. Borrowed Influence comes from title, position, or status. Earned Influence comes from adding value to and building trust with others. Both are important to your success, and by the end of this book you'll understand how each type of influence will help you succeed.

I've had clients say things like, "It isn't fair. Why should I have to build my influence? I should be measured on my merits." All I can say to this is, yes, it should be different. And yes, you should be measured on your merits, just like you were when you applied for and attended college. It was an even playing field, which is why women are 57% of college graduates. But the workforce is not an even playing field. I wouldn't have a job as a coach and consultant, or be writing this book if things were the way they *should* be. I'm endeavoring to help you deal with what is, and what is, is pervasive inequity across numerous sectors. That's why you need influence.

There are a few more reasons why it is important for you to build your influence.

First, you have a ton to offer. Your strengths are needed in the world today. When we look at the things that are going wrong in our communities, our organizations, and our governments, it's often the female strengths that are missing. The world needs you. Now.

Second, competence is only a fraction of what it takes to succeed. As unfortunate as it is, you are likely, at some point in your career, to see someone get hired or promoted who was not qualified. How did this person get hired or promoted if they were not qualified? Usually it's because they had some type of influence. That's what you need.

Third, nobody at the top who has achieved anything meaningful has done it alone. We all need help and support from others. Influence gets you that support.

Lastly, you need influence to overcome roadblocks. Road-blocks are those people who don't like you and want to throw marbles in your path. Some of my clients find the notion that not everyone will like them pretty hard to take. So, I respond with the question, "Do you like everybody?" Admittedly, I do not like everybody, so why would I expect everybody to like me? Also, there are likely to be people you come across who are jealous of your talents, or who are competitive. Maybe they just don't have good values like you do. If you have engaged in some well-placed efforts to build relationships with your roadblocks and it is not working, you will need influence. I'll show you how to get that influence and use it to move on down the road.

Now that you know why you need influence, we'll move on to the importance of cultivating the mindset of an influenc-er—or always thinking of yourself as "Your Name, Inc." Very few professionals have this mindset, which it why it's one of the biggest advantages you can give yourself.

To gain the mindset of an influencer, all you have to do is shift your focus from how a company meets your needs to how you, as "Your Name, Inc." will add benefit to any place you work. This becomes your personal brand and when you are always focused on giving your best and delivering what your "client" (your boss/company) needs, you will have a winning mindset that sets you apart from others and ensures your success. If you are always filling a need (your client/boss's need), you will always have a job. If you don't know what your client needs, it's time to ask.

As mentioned, one of the reasons that women are not more

prevalent in leadership positions is because we often are playing a different game than men are playing. Throughout the book, and through case studies, I'm going to show you how using your strengths can align with some of the strategies and tactics that men have been using for decades, and how, used together with your female strengths, they are exponentially powerful.

Having said that, I need to also say that there will also be situations when you have to move on. This is about discernment, about being able to assess when, despite your most diligent efforts, the odds are too stacked against your desired outcome. I've moved on more than once when I could see that people in high places were not seeing me in the right light. Sometimes it will take you too long to gain the influence you need to change the circumstances. In those cases, your career and sanity are best served by finding a different job. Remember, the strategies I'm going to share work most of the time, but not all of the time. Sometimes, you just have to move on to a fresh environment.

Right now, I'm going to reveal what your strengths are. As you look at them, I want you to reserve judgment. They may be triggering at first, especially if you have been criticized for having one of these strengths. If that is the case, I apologize for anyone who gave you that false impression. These truly are your *strengths*, and when used strategically are an invaluable asset to you. I built an entire career, overcame the biggest challenge of my life, had huge successes and advancement; in other words, I completely accomplished my goals, and continue to accomplish all my goals, all by building my influence with these strengths, and you can too. I'm going to show you how to use them, so be a sponge, sit back, and enjoy learning about just how powerful you really are!

Ready?

Your 5 innate female strengths are:
Giving
Emoting
Leveraging
Delivering
Bouncing Back

Remember to keep that open mind! Now we're going to move into understanding these strengths, how you can use them to build your influence, and be inspired to leverage them, knowing that the keys to your success are already within you!

"Giving is better than receiving
because giving starts the receiving process"
~ Jim Rohn

Chapter 1
Giving

Giving is by far your most important strength because it is the foundation every other strength depends and builds upon. Giving is the basis for building strong relationships. And strong relationships with the right people are what build your influence.

The definition of giving, for our purposes, is:

An action or gesture from one individual to another (or from one individual to a group of individuals) that adds some type of value (in the eyes of the receiver).

It's important to note that the receiver defines what is valuable, not us. Therefore, if we want to be successful in using giving to build strong relationships, we have to understand what the receiver values and wants, so we can give it to them.

I'm not the first person to identify giving as integral to great relationships. Dr. Willard F. Harley Jr., a marriage and family therapist out of Minneapolis, identifies giving in his book *His Needs, Her Needs* as the primary basis for a healthy marriage. He discusses the concept of the "love bank." When we give, we make "deposits" into the love bank that grow exponentially. These deposits feed and nurture the relationship, and grow to a point where we can draw on them when we need to.

This isn't all that different from the types of relationships you are going to build through your strength of giving. You can call it whatever you want—the friendship bank, the comradery bank, the rapport bank—the result is the same. It builds connection and trust, which are the basis of any good relationship. And when the account is filled up over time, you can draw upon it for your own needs.

I'm sure we can all agree that most women are innate givers. In fact, I would argue that as the childbearing gender, we are hardwired to nurture others. I mean, let's face it, we were chosen to birth humanity! You were designed to give the ultimate gift—life itself—so whether you have children or not giving is in your DNA.

You might be thinking, "I give a lot, and it's exhausting me!" Believe me, I understand. Sometimes we *do* give too much. We give until it hurts, with limited or no reciprocation, because we're "supposed to" or in order to be a "good" wife, mother, employee, daughter, et cetera. Maybe we feel obligated to give to "make things work." When we over-give, it can be exhausting and demoralizing. It can drain the life out of us, especially when people come to expect a level of giving from us that goes beyond our time and energy capabilities, or that requires us to sacrifice our own self-care. It's especially taxing when the giving is not reciprocal.

When we get in the habit of giving too much we create that dynamic within our relationships. People's baseline experience of us is as an over-giver. We've trained them to see it as normal and maybe even to depend on it, while we feel increasingly stuck in this role. And when we start to modulate and pull back our giving to a more realistic level, the recipient(s) of this over-giving may react negatively, which can make us question our decision to make ourselves a priority. How do I know? Because I've done it.

Giving too much in this way keeps us from reaching our full potential. Why? Because we are tapped out. Spent. Exhausted. In this over-giving state, we are not using our strength of giving to our advantage; we cannot fully contribute or be our best.

Most people have strengths that they can lean on to succeed. But, as in the case of giving, strengths can be overused, or used in the wrong context, and that's how we get into trouble. Here's an example of a personal asset becoming a liability. When a football player exerts force on the football field to win a play, he is using his bodily strength and force for good—to win the game for his team. When that same bodily strength is used in the wrong context, however, like using force to win an argument at home with his wife, it becomes a liability. What he has come to lean on for success may be the very thing that will make him unsuccessful in his marriage. Same strength, different context.

It is the same of giving. This powerful female strength can and will help you create the success and advancement you crave. The trick is to use it in a balanced way, in the right context, and strategically so that it's healthy and reciprocated.

This means that we must stop carrying a disproportionate load of giving in our relationships. If we can learn the balancing act of healthy giving, it actually energizes us. It makes us feel powerful. And we attain that power by developing only reciprocal giving relationships, ones in which we receive benefits commensurate with our contributions.

Now, you might think strategic giving is selfish...but is it? Absolutely not. First of all, men have been doing it for years. It's part of what keeps them at the top. They don't give randomly or broadly. They give where it counts in business. We have to play the same game to win our positions in leadership; we have to leverage our strength strategically, like men do.

Second, strategic giving is not selfish because reciprocity is the basis of healthy relationships. I like to call them "give–give" relationships, because both parties give and both parties receive value. There is no "give and take" in a healthy relationship. Giving is a gesture that moves a relationship forward. Taking is a gesture that moves a relationship backward. So, seeking a give/give relationship with someone that has something of value to offer you is not selfish; it's smart.

There are some obvious exceptions to the reciprocal giving standard. Childrearing, caregiving for an elderly or sick family member, and volunteering are all examples of one-way giving. The important thing to remember is that we choose to do these things because something in our heart is fulfilled from it. Or, we may choose it because we feel an obligation to our family member. The point is, when we choose this type of one-way giving relationship, we usually gain a sort of psychological and/or emotional benefit from doing it, especially if giving in these ways represents a part of our values. This is healthy, as long as we recognize that it is a choice and take time for our own self-care.

So never feel guilty about making sure you receive reciprocal energy and benefit in your relationships. If it's not a give/give situation, then it's not a healthy relationship (barring the exceptions we just discussed). If you are not getting commensurate benefit from your giving, you should consider discontinuing that relationship.

There is one last exception to the reciprocal, give–give

relationship standard. This is when you are cultivating a new strategic relationship with an influencer who might not ordinarily be in your life but you have strategically targeted as someone who can help you in your career.

The definition of an influencer, for our purposes, is:

> *A person who inspires or guides the actions of others; often a person that is able to generate interest in something.*

To start building these types of relationships, you are going to give first and give for a while in an effort to build trust with people who can benefit you in the long term.

In business, giving is the new commodity. It's no longer "Ask, and you shall receive," but "Give, and you shall receive." In fact, giving is such an important action in relationship-building that more and more corporations are embracing a "give first" model as part of their company values and marketing strategies. They realize that giving first builds trust in their brand, and they are finding ways to give value before attempting to make a sale.

As famous author, thought leader, and corporate leadership trainer Jim Rohn once said, "Giving is better than receiving because giving starts the receiving process."

That's what we are counting on when we give in order to build a new strategic relationship with an influencer. Eventually, these relationships should become reciprocal; if they don't, it may be time to move on to another influencer.

So how do you do it? How do you start giving to build key relationships that will help you advance and reach your goals? How do you give first, and then receive?

The strategy to get started is just 3 simple steps.

1.   Identify your goal(s)
2.   List influencers who can help you reach those goals
3.   Choose 3 to 5 influencers to build relationships with

You have to decide which influencers you will strategically target and build relationships with. Again, this isn't selfish; it is smart and strategic. It also allows you to set up a healthy, reciprocal, give-give relationship.

Create a list of influencers in your field who have the potential to help you. Some you may already know, or know of; finding others may take some time and research.

Open up a Word document or get a piece of paper and a pen and write down answers to these questions.

1.   What are your goals? You need to know where you want to go before you can identify who has the ability to help you get there. One approach is, if everything were perfect in your life, if you were living the life of your dreams, what would that look like? If you know that, then you know what your goal is and, unless you are very close to reaching it, you'll want to list out step-goals. Step-goals are the progressive steps that lead up to your ultimate goal. For instance, if you eventually want to become the CEO of a company and are now in middle management, step-goals might include becoming a Director, then a C-suite executive, and so on. If you are some-

one who wants to leave the future open because things can change so much over time, your approach might be to write down what you want to achieve in the next eighteen months. This eighteen-month goal will give you something on which to base your next step in finding influencers that can help you get there. If another timeframe works better, choose that. The point is, you need something to shoot for before you can figure out who can help you get there. So figure out the goal you are shooting for.

2. Next, think about the influencers with the ability and influence to help you achieve your goals. Ask yourself:

   a. Who has achieved my goal?
   b. Who does everyone listen to in my field?
   c. Who does everyone follow in my field?
   d. Who has massive influence in my field?
   e. Who do my roadblocks need/respect?
   f. Who has access to influencers?

   Remember, "roadblocks" are people standing in your way. They may be jealous coworkers or competitive colleagues. Maybe it's someone in leadership. If you have tried to build a relationship with a roadblock and that strategy has not worked, then you'll have to influence around them. Think of people that they need, respect, and want to please. Add those people to your list of influencers.

Continue to tally up the movers and shakers—the people who, if you had a relationship with them, could give you a leg up or even carry you. Who could give you good advice or mentoring? People who have already reached your goal are always good influencers because they can share with you how they achieved success. You don't have to reinvent the wheel—you just have to tap into their wisdom and follow their path.

Again, it may take some time and research to complete this list. If you're not sure who the influencers are, ask someone who would know or just start googling.

Once you have this list, you'll likely find people on it who are not readily accessible to you. That's okay; in fact I like to encourage women to reach high, because the higher they reach the higher they will go. This is where Step 3 comes in.

3. Your third step is to add people to your list who have access to your influencers. They may make it easier for you to build a relationship with them right now, or at least have the potential to make an introduction later. Don't rule out people like executive assistants, family members, employees, or friends of your influencer. Add these people to your list.

Don't be discouraged if you look at your list and find most of them are in the "access to influencers" category. If one of your influencers is Richard Branson, for instance, you can't help but list an access-to influencer alongside his name. It may take some extra time and effort, but eventually it will lead to an introduction, or a meeting, or an email address—similar to the game "Six Degrees of Kevin Bacon."

What's cool is there's a critical mass in this work. A lot of influencers hang out together. Once you get the hang of this and make it a way of life, you'll create a momentum that grows. I know this from experience: once I had access to one influencer it often opened the door for many more.

Having said that, don't overlook people who *are* more accessible to you. You might write down your own boss, or your boss's boss. You may be close to someone in your work environment who has achieved a promotion that you want to earn some day. Put them on your influencer list. Bottom line: your influencer list cannot be too long. Add to it and refresh it regularly. This is not something you throw together and put in a drawer; it's part of your ongoing career strategy. It's a living, breathing document that will change and morph as your career changes and grows.

Now that you have your list of influencers, think of your goals and ask yourself, "Of all these people, who are the most likely to help me achieve my goals? Who has enough influence to pick up the phone and get results?" Put a star by their name.

Look for people who have a track record of "sponsoring" others. What I mean by "sponsor" is going to bat for other people—such as making a phone call on their behalf—even if it means taking a risk. You may not know this upfront, but try to find out because the most powerful influencer is someone who is willing to do something proactively for you.

Now take your lists and look at the names you put stars by. Circle three to five of them to focus on first. There's no magic to the three-to-five range; I suggest this because building relationships takes time and effort, and you don't have all the time in the world. You have to pick and choose.

If everyone on your list is high profile and hard to reach, you'll get frustrated trying to build a legitimate connection to them all at once. Therefore, most of your short list should be people who are easier to reach, along with one long shot (your "Richard Branson"). Try to pick people who can have the most benefit to you, and/or that bring a number of benefits with them (i.e. they are respected as a leader AND tend to sponsor others). Ideally, the majority of them should be people you can start working on building a relationship with right now. Look for someone with who you may have something in common, as this will make the initial outreach and connection a bit easier.

This short list of influencers becomes your roadmap—the people with whom you are going to deliberately build strategic relationships.

It's likely that you will start working on some people, only to later uncover that they are not the best fit for you. Maybe you learn that they will not be helpful (I learned that someone I was working on actually had a reputation for undermining women, so I stopped my relationship-building efforts with her). Or, maybe they lose their influence (this happens with politicians a lot), or maybe you find your values don't match (i.e. you learn they have some shady ways of doing business); Maybe you realize that they are not willing to help others at all. Whatever the case, refer back to your longer list when this happens so you can choose a more productive influencer to work on.

Now, back to your short list of three to five influencers.

You will start by using your strength of giving to build interest and connection, followed by trust and, ultimately, reciprocity. Remember, that while your goal is to develop an actual, give/give relationship with them, it's not going to start that way. You are going to give first for a while. This is not "Ask, and you shall receive"; it's "Give, and you shall receive." So, you are going to follow this very smart business strategy and give first.

While compiling this list, you should have done some research on what your influencers might want. After all, it's really hard to give if you don't know what to give, or have the opportunity to give. You also don't want to scare off your influencer by giving too much too soon. You have to dip your toe in the water before you can jump in and start swimming. You have to intelligently assess the best way to start. That's why the research is so important.

Find out as much as you can about your influencers. What makes them tick? What do they care about? Where do they live? Family? Friends? Hobbies? Favorite sports teams, food, entertainers, et cetera? Accomplishments? Passions? Obstacles they've overcome? Their path to success? Their climb to the top? Business philosophies? Leadership style? What values do they have? Find out as much information as you possibly can about them, and look for a nexus between that information and what you are capable of giving.

As mentioned, there are two main ways to do this research: through other people and via the Internet. Thanks to technology, we have oceans of information at our fingertips, so just type the influencer's name in a search engine and read everything that comes up. Then, mine their social media accounts and ask people who know them or have access to them. Pay particular attention to where their life experiences, values and interests intersect with your own. This type of nexus is where you can really give with a depth of sincerity that comes naturally to you.

I've found that for many women, doing this part of the work brings up the question: "What could I possibly have to offer an influencer?" What you have to remember is, influencers are people too. They have emotional needs, intellectual needs, and the human need for connection. Just because you don't have the position, title, or influence they have doesn't mean you can't give something that they will truly value and connect with.

Think of the people you are closest to. Why are you close with them? Chances are it's not that they send you a Christmas card, or show up at your house for a party. Sure, that's nice, but if you were to really soul search, the people you are closest to—the people you value the most—are providing you some type of emotional or moral support. You like being around them because they make you feel good. You feel connected with them. You feel they "get you." They feed your soul. They demonstrate they are out for your best interests, so you trust them.

That is what we are after in our relationship-building. We want to feed the soul of our influencers, and not in a fake or superficial way. As I said in the introduction, your work is to find a sincere way to do it; to find a nexus between what you can give authentically and what is meaningful to their soul.

In his book *Social: Why Our Brains Are Hard Wired To Connect*, UCLA professor and neuroscientist Matthew Lieberman takes into account over a thousand studies that essentially prove human connection is as important to our survival as food, water, and shelter. Our brains are actually hardwired for it.

This is evidenced by the increase in depression and suicide during the Covid19 lockdowns. People are starved for connection. We cannot live without it. This is why it makes sense to feed the soul of your influencer. You can fulfill this need for connection.

As far as I can tell, and from my experience, there seems to be six areas of giving, all of which correlate to our basic emotional needs. These needs can translate into things that we can do for, or give to, others in order to build a relationship with them.

The six areas of giving are:

1. <u>Help</u>: Help me reach a goal of mine
2. <u>Recognition</u>: Recognize, affirm, validate, or appreciate me
3. <u>Connection</u>: Express warmth, interest, *listen, listen, listen* to me, demonstrate you understand me
4. <u>Time</u>: Spend time with me, or on a project I care about
5. <u>Gifts</u>: Give me a gift I'd appreciate or do a nice gesture for me
6. <u>Support</u>: Be there in my time of need or celebration

When it comes to giving, perhaps the most important thing you can do is listen. There's a lot of talk today about "finding your voice," being heard, breaking the silence, and stepping out into the world with your ideas. While I do believe it's important for women to find their voice (men often have loud voices and we need to have a voice too), there's far too much sounding off without the proper consideration of others. Consequently, there's a lot of screaming going on, and not enough of the very thing that will bring people together—listening.

Listening is a huge relationship-building skill for two reasons. People love it when we shut our mouth and listen to them, rather than hijacking the conversation with our own story. Listening without interruption makes people feel valued. Even more important (and often overlooked) is that when you listen you'll find that people will tell you what they need.

Here's an example from my own life: I met an influential woman I knew I was going to build a relationship with. As we spoke (or, more accurately, she spoke and I listened), I noticed that most of what she said involved sharing recognition and accolades she'd received. It was easy to see that she valued recognition. Recognition fed her soul. So, I gave her that every chance I got.

If someone values family a lot, you'll want to make your giving and conversations revolve around that value. If someone is always talking about who did them wrong, then you'll want to empathize with them around that experience. If someone is always talking about a problem, see if you can empathize and also bring a needed resource or solution to the table so that you're helping to alleviate their pain point.

It's actually really easy if you just focus on listening. When you listen, you get valuable information that reveals what your influencer values and cares about. Then you can more accurately gauge the appropriate ways to give that build connection and trust.

So how do these areas of giving work in practical application? I found that what worked with some influencers did not work with others. For instance, I was able to help certain influencers reach their goals (Help), but with others it was more beneficial to spend time with them or on a project they cared about (Time), or supporting them in their time of need or celebration (Support). For some, I was able to utilize several categories at once.

You may or may not know what types of giving resonate with certain influencers. If it's the latter, you have to start by doing your research, then gingerly try something that looks like it should work. You have to dip your toe in the water gently, do the initial giving, and then note the response.

Maybe you found out they like the café au lait at Starbucks. You can set up a meeting with them and bring them one (Gifts); then during the meeting express your truthful appreciation and praise of something they did that positively impacted you (Recognition).

If you're working remotely, you might have their favorite cup of coffee delivered to them just in time for your virtual coffee meeting? (Gifts) That would surely show some effort and get their attention. You might even say in your virtual meeting, "I know you're very busy and I really appreciate the twenty minutes you are giving me today. I wanted to send you your favorite cup of coffee. It was the least I could do to thank you for your time." (Recognition)

Once you've done that, note the response of your influencer. If there is a warm and appreciative response, you judged well and it's likely you are safe to move on to planning your next giving opportunity.

Here's an example. I learned that one of my influencers held an annual leukemia fundraiser after losing a relative to the disease. I attended the fundraiser (Recognition & Time), and donated a bottle of wine for auction (Gifts). I also made sure it was one of his favorite wines so he'd take notice (Connection), and wrote a little note letting him know I made the donation to acknowledge his amazing leadership in raising funds for the cure (Support). Later in our relationship, he reciprocated by supporting me in various ways.

In my last CEO position most of the influencers were political figures. They valued exposure on social media, so I would share their posts on Facebook or make positive comments about them. This was highly meaningful to them because it gave them greater exposure and recognized and validated them (Help, Recognition & Support).

I've started an amazing amount of influencer relationships just by liking, sharing, and commenting on their social media posts. In fact, this was one of the primary strategies I used to gain access to them. You can do this too. If you want to get the attention of an influencer who is also a public figure, try commenting on and sharing their posts consistently. It gives you direct access to them.

You don't have to find out a ton of information about someone to make a connection. One time I was helping a client make a connection with a health club executive she was not getting any response from. She reached out for a year via email and phone messages and he never responded. When we started working together, we mined his social media, which was actually pretty sparse—we gained very little information other than he was the grandfather of two. Well, the client I was working with served children, which meant there was a nexus between what he cared about and what she did. We were able to craft an email that subtly connected to him as a grandfather (Recognition & Connection). That email, and the subsequent giving to build the relationship, resulted in her getting the contract she was seeking with the health club. And she could not have done it without him.

I want to stop here for a minute and talk about recognition. Remember when I talked about meaningful relationships feeding our soul? Well, nothing feeds the soul more than validation and recognition. It shows that you are on the right track (despite your occasional doubts) and that your good work and brilliance has been noticed by others. Or, maybe it's validation that something really sucks—along with the warmth and connection that comes from someone who expresses understanding and empathy. For most people I know, even the most successful and confident, validation and sincere recognition have a significantly positive impact.

So, one way that you can continually feed the soul of others is to give sincere recognition, broadly and often. You might be thinking, *Why would an influencer care what I think?*, but you'd be amazed at how many people leave out the niceties with high-powered influencers. Often people don't bother to validate influencers because they assume these high-powered folks hear it all the time—or don't need the support.

Another scenario is that accolades come frequently to the influencer, but they come from people who are just saying these things to get in good favor with them. This type of insincere, self-serving motivation is easy to detect, so make sure your recognition is authentic and heartfelt.

Another way to recognize someone is to hold the elevator or door for them (yes—that actually surprises a lot of people, because so few do it.). It's a kind gesture focused on the wellbeing of another person. You are recognizing they exist and showing you care (Recognition & Connection). And it's so simple!

How about this? I used to walk up to my yoga instructor after every class, look her in the eye and say thank you. I did this after every class. Nobody else did; they just waved and shouted thanks as they hurriedly ran out the door. My extra effort—which took only about twenty seconds out of my day— conveyed sincere appreciation of the value she provided to me. After I made this a habit, the instructor made it a point to give me a few extra tips and a little extra attention in the class. The takeaway here? Take the time to watch what a group of people *aren't* doing for an influencer, and fill that gap. It works.

Below is another example from my own life. I think something like this works better for mid-career women, because you can get away with a little bit of verbal banter when you have a more established career under your belt.

At one point I was working with a number of men who were older than me, and I knew that many of them thought of themselves as old. So I started calling them "young man." I would see them in the hall and say, "How are you doing today, young man?" I wanted to give to them the idea that their age didn't matter; that anyone can be young. I think it gave them a lift. It made them feel good and even more vital. Many of them would laugh, or blush a bit and say thank you. I nearly always got a positive response. They loved it, and I still do it to this day. In fact, I tried it with a woman the other day in a restaurant, and she gushed with appreciation. Giving in these small ways has a huge impact, if you make it a habit. And, if you feel you are in a position to get away with this, feel free to steal it!

I'm going through all these examples to get your creative juices flowing about the myriad of ways you can give to start building a relationship with your influencers. It takes time to think through, but it's well worth it. And in the process, you'll be increasing your own influence (Earned Influence).

Now, let's start talking about your first contact with your influencer. You have a number of choices on how to do this, based on what you've researched and learned about this person. Here are some of the most common:

Email

Phone call

Social media

Gathering/meeting

Event

You also have to be clear about your goal for that first contact. Are you trying to get a meeting? If so, what reason can you come up with that would persuade the influencer to take that meeting? For example, do you want to interview them about how they achieved their success? What are the top two or three points you want to focus on in your initial discussion? Influencers are busy, so you want to get to the point and show them you won't waste their time. And make sure your questions are not something that you can easily find the answer to on the internet. Ask intelligent, thoughtful business questions that your influencers are well-positioned to answer. That's how you use their time wisely and make yourself stand out. It's all about striking a balance—you want to spend enough time that the conversation has some depth, but not so long that you are jamming up their day. The goal is for them to notice you, and want to continue interacting with you after the meeting.

Maybe the first contact is an email, a card, or a letter. Yes, I said a letter. Given all the electronic communication these days, a letter, especially a handwritten one, will really stand out. My husband and I get handwritten postcards from a friend of ours a few times a year, and I'm always deeply touched by the extra time and effort.

Another way to start the ball rolling is to show up at an event you know the influencer is attending and bump into them. If and when you do this, have a strategy in place. For example, if one of the people on your list has access to the influencer, reach out to them ahead of time and ask them to make an introduction. Then, once you have your influencer's eyes and ears, have your opener rehearsed. What will you say that aligns with their values—because you've learned what their values are from your research, right?

The main point to remember is to start slow and gentle, note their response, and evaluate your next move based on that response. Everyone has different privacy preferences. Everyone has different boundary sensitivities. You want to be on the lookout for those cues as you dip your toe in the water of building this relationship. Think of your closest friends—I'll bet that some of those relationships took longer to deepen than others. That's because of the differences in each friend.

When you look at it from this perspective, you can appreciate that your initial and subsequent moves will be different for each influencer. There is no right or wrong. There's simply what works and what doesn't, so let their responses be your guide.

If your influencer has reached a goal that you would like to reach, try to get a meeting as a chance to be mentored. For a lot of influencers, being asked to mentor really resonates (fulfills an emotional need); it makes them feel good to be recognized for their expertise and know they are helping the next round of leaders. So you see, these relationships can be give-give from the start. You receive great advice and wisdom from them, and they get an emotional need met by you.

If you do this, have your second contact with the influencer planned out before the *first* meeting. Have a list of questions, and make sure they relate to something you are or will be doing. This way, after your influencer shares their wise counsel, you can tell them you are working on a related project and ask if you can reach out to them for feedback in the future.

Most influencers will find it very hard to say no to this. In fact, they will be expecting to hear from you again, which is what you want. Don't leave that first interaction without thinking through and solidifying what your next touch point with them will be. And after that first meeting, send a handwritten thank you card. Almost nobody does this. Do it and set yourself apart.

After your second interaction, you keep going with a third, a fourth, and so on. Before you know it, and as long as you keep giving, you will be growing a reciprocal, give/give relationship with them.

While doing this work be sure to think long term, because you want to build relationships *before* you need them. When

I built my new nonprofit, I found myself leveraging relationships I had been building through giving for three years. My
influencers already trusted me and my personal brand. My
reputation as a giver was solid, and that made people want
to give when I needed them in a crisis.

We'll discuss how to tell when you can really lean on these
relationships later in the book. For now, you've got all you
need to start the process of giving to build relationships with
influential people who can help you achieve your goals.

So let's recap giving.

- Giving is the key to building strong relationships,
  and it is an innate female strength.
- There is a right and wrong way to utilizing your
  giving strength. Only reciprocal, give/give relationships are healthy. But you'll have to give for
  a while during the building phase of a new influencer relationship.
- Engage in research to identify your influencers
  and those who have access to them. Also, research the interests and passions of those influencers so you use your strength of giving to fulfill
  their needs and build trusting relationships.
- Remember that each relationship, and the sensitivities of those involved, are different. Nobody
  likes a "creeper" who oversteps or gets too close
  too quickly. Dip your toe in the water first, note
  the response, and take it from there. Again, do
  your research on your influencers so you can

come up with simple ways to initiate contact and start giving in a way that builds trust over time and becomes a reciprocal relationship that can bring value to you as well.

- Brainstorm a good first-time method of contact and giving gesture. Remember to give first, before you need the relationship; that way, when you do need help you'll have a support system already in place.

- If you don't get a response after several well-placed attempts, move on to another influencer. Not everyone will respond. You don't need everyone, so that's okay.

- Utilized strategically, giving can be the most powerful strength you have. Once you realize this power, you will be addicted to using it to spread good will and build your own influence.

To help you gain a deeper understanding of giving and how integral it is to building influential relationships, I've included some case studies of people I know who have successfully built healthy, reciprocal relationships with influencers that they were later able to leverage to achieve a goal.

When you're done with those, we'll move on to Emoting.

Case Study 1
Stacy: Landing Her Target Job

Stacy was a brilliant young woman who wanted a job with a certain company. She did her homework and found out that the person who oversaw the job she wanted taught an exercise class in the morning before work. In order to build a relationship with this person, Stacy signed up for the same exercise class, and utilized the time before and after class to engage this person in pleasant conversation. She gave to her by showing appreciation for the class. She gave her verbal recognition for the positive impact the exercise class was having on her health and life. Over time, Stacy was able to discern things they had in common, and was able to start working that into their short talks, which built more rapport.

Slowly, Stacy also found a way to work their professional lives into the conversation, thereby giving the influencer information about her job experience. It wasn't an "in your face" approach. It was subtle and gradual, with casual remarks here and there eventually blossoming into longer conversations.

Eventually, the job Stacy wanted opened up. By this time, the influencer knew her well and they had built a rapport. When the time came to advertise the coveted job, guess who was invited to interview, and later got the position? This type of approach takes patience, thought and time, but wouldn't you say it was worth it for Stacy to reach her goal?

Case Study 2
The Sports Exec

I wanted to build a relationship with a certain professional sports executive. I had been able to dig up his email address through my connections, but that's where my luck ended. I emailed him for almost a year with no response.

At one point, I saw in the news that his team had acquired a new player, and they were hopeful this player would be a game changer for the team. I don't know much about sports, so I asked a sports savvy colleague about it. I got some good information and then crafted a carefully worded email congratulating this executive for the acquisition of this great new player. I shared my hopes and confidence that it would bring a higher level of success to the team.

Now I wasn't someone that this person was going to naturally gravitate toward for several reasons, not the least of which was that he didn't need anyone like me in his circle. But I found a way to give that was meaningful to him, that touched an emotion in him and that aligned with his values.

And guess what? I got an immediate response and shortly afterward we had our first meeting. One meeting turned into several, and eventually I was able to get this sports organization invested in my organization, which was my goal.

I want you to know that I did not put the information I got from my colleague into that initial email. I only spoke to my colleague in order to understand the background (the exec's attempts to acquire the player) so I could express sincerity in my email. I wanted to feel the energy of the excitement so that it came off in my email. The note itself was short, sweet, and congratulatory.

It's important to note that I probably would not have gotten the immediate response had I waited a day or two. The buzz was happening now. It was in the paper and everyone was reacting to it. I had to move while the emotions were high and the excitement was in the air. If you have an opportunity like this, don't wait. To really connect, you have to be there for them in their time of celebration.

That simple email is what started the ball rolling. We developed a reciprocal relationship that I was able to leverage many times, and I was able to give to him value through my professional contacts. Win-Win! Give-Give! That's how it works.

Case Study 3
Rice Crispy Treats

This is one of my favorites. In my last CEO job, I was pretty busy. Because I worked with elected officials, anyone who had an interest in influencing public policy wanted a piece of my time. Fortunately, I had an assistant who was vigilant about protecting my time. There was a man who made continual requests—most of them that didn't meet my "Yes, I'll take that meeting" criteria—so my assistant would say no before it even got to me.

One day she came into my office and said, "Lacy, I know that you don't want meetings like this, but I just learned that you and this guy have a close mutual friend." She gave me the name of my friend, who was also a business colleague for whom I had high regard. If the man requesting the meeting was also friends with this person, well then, I would take the meeting. That was the first thing he did right. He connected himself to someone I respected and had a relationship with in his conversation with my assistant. (This is leveraging and we'll discuss this more later).

It was the second thing he did, however, that brought us even closer. He showed up to our first meeting with my favorite dessert as a gift. Not just one, but a whole box of rice crispy squares. What impressed me most was that I don't exactly advertise that I like them. In fact, I'm pretty sure nobody knew because at the time I was on a pretty strict low-carb diet. My assistant didn't even know, so I'm not sure how he found out. Suffice it to say I immediately knew that this guy had done some deep digging. I appreciated that and we had an immediate rapport.

Now, I'm not a pushover. Far from it. I've been known to tell my staff that a "healthy paranoia about other people's intensions is a wise and good thing." I also believe the axiom "Just because someone acts nice, doesn't mean they are nice." But when this man entered my office and gave me the treats, he came off as sincere. He also knew some things about my accomplishments and even my goals. He was really able to show his value to me by proposing a way to help me reach one of those goals, and he did this in a very genuine way. He started off with giving.

The end of the meeting was really the beginning—the beginning of a valued relationship that I still have to this day. I fully acknowledge that while this person is a man, he was leveraging every female strength in getting my attention and gaining my trust. He delivered and never backed down from his sincerity. Kudos to him! That's how it's done.

Case Study 4
Losing the Contract

I also have an example of what can happen in the absence of such a relationship. When I was sharing the outline for this book with several of my "Female Friends Community" I was told this story:

"Lacy, I wish I'd had this wisdom last year. I lost a contract with a company that was my bread and butter. I had a great relationship with one executive, but I never made the effort to know the guy above him (the COO). I had access to the COO, but I just didn't think I needed to make the effort. One day, the CEO left and the COO was hired to replace him. When he stepped into the CEO position, the recession hit and he wanted to save money. He immediately let go any contractor that he didn't know, which included me. I was heartbroken, because I knew that my contract might have been saved if I'd had a relationship with him. But because he'd never heard of me, he didn't know my value, so I was cut. I think I could have prevented that if I'd built a relationship with him. As it stands now, he won't return my calls because he doesn't even know me."

Let the above be your cautionary tale. Spending the time and effort to build relationships now will ensure that you have a support system when you need it. It's like insurance. Start now.

Case Study 5
A One-Sided Ask

This is an example of someone asking for support before they've earned trust. I have long been committed to offering this support to help women achieve success, which is why I started building my community of "Female Friends." I share with them the techniques and strategies that I used to over-come competitive women and discriminatory men and break through barriers and, consequently, I've built a good base of followers and coaching clients. Interacting with and helping these women has been incredibly fulfilling for me—in other words, it is a wonderful reciprocal relationship.

That said, I also get regular requests from people I don't know asking me to promote their conference, their book, or their program. They are usually people who have not put in the blood, sweat, and tears that I have put in to build a following and create deep value for clients, yet here they are, asking to leverage my hard work without offering me any value in return.

The question is, why would I share their products and ser-vices with my following? If I did that, I'd be endorsing some-thing I'm not even sure is a good product. I don't know this person and they have not offered me any value in return, so why should I believe they would offer value to my following?

This is a classic example of a request for a "take" with no give. I don't know them. I don't trust them. I ignore their email.

Now, let's suppose they had come to me with a give—some-thing that brings value to my business. Maybe they ask me to be on their podcast to promote my coaching, and the podcast has a wide distribution that will bring broader awareness of my value to women. Then let's say I get to interact with their brand and it's good stuff. It builds my trust in the quality of their work, as well as their sincerity. They've shown me that they have value to offer. And if they continue to make an effort to build a giving relationship with me, I'll be a lot more likely to reciprocate and promote their product to my following. That's how it works. They gave first, now they receive.

Never just go to someone cold turkey and ask them to help you. Nobody owes us anything, especially if they don't even know us. You must always offer value first, even if that value is merely some recognition, warmth, or a trusted friendship that provides your influencer some emotional support.

*"The best and most beautiful things in the world
cannot be seen or even touched.
They must be felt with the heart"
~ Hellen Keller*

Chapter 2
Emoting

In this chapter, we'll discuss why emoting is important to human beings in general, as well as the most and least effective ways to use your emotion. I'll also show you how you can use negative events to leverage your emoting strength, and how most great leaders constructively use emoting to establish their brand as a strong leader.

For our purposes, the definition of emoting is:

To express oneself with passion and forward momentum.

Note in particular the words "forward momentum." This is a key point in the chapter, and I'll get to why in just a bit.

As in the case of giving, many women are surprised to find that emoting is a valuable strength for their toolkit. If you're one of those women, I think I know why.

You have been told you are too emotional in the workplace, or

You notice that people are generally monotone and associate being emotional with being weak.

Have you ever tried to tamp down or minimize your feelings at work because you feared expressing your emotions would jeopardize your success?

Unfortunately, our workplace experience often seems to be teaching us that our emotions are not welcome. But that's not exactly true.

Let me share how I learned that emotions are important in a professional setting, when leveraged in the right context.

Years ago, I was addressing a business problem with my board of directors and my emotion leaked out into my presentation. I had trained myself to be so "objective," because I'd learned that female emotion is not welcome in the workplace. In fact, I'd learned that it identifies you as irrational and weak. By that point, however, I had become so frustrated with the matter on which I was presenting that I could no longer hold it in.

I ended the presentation believing I had just made a colossal mistake; instead, I ended up getting most of what I wanted. In fact, a male board member—and one of my influencers—later approached me and said, "Lacy, always speak to us that way. You made me believe in something today." I mean - Wow! After that, I started to reconsider my assumptions about emoting.

What I figured out is that it's *undirected, negative emotion* that loses the day. Well-placed emotion, combined with a forward direction and positive solution, is not only welcome, it's desired.

I got the support I needed that day by making a compelling motivational speech. And I didn't even realize that's what I was doing. I was in the moment, emoting about a problem, then beseeching my audience to implement a solution—and it was effective!

The experience was eye-opening, and I was determined to figure out why it worked. I spent a lot of time reflecting and researching, and here's the conclusion I came to:

Expressing emotion cannot be used to badmouth, speculate,

complain, tear down; lament mistakes or bad deeds, or express victimization or fearmongering. It also cannot be focused on anger, hate, resentment, or anything personal. Oftentimes this type of emoting is scary to others; other times it is seen merely as unwanted drama, with any nugget of truth slipping through the cracks and falling on deaf ears. Why? Because this sort of emotion looks backward, without offering any solution.

To be successful, emotion must be expressed in a way that moves us forward, toward a positive outcome. It starts with how things can or should be different, how a pain or burden can be lifted. And if you add to that a vision for a solution—how it would or could work—that's even better.

For example, you can emote about a disappointment, problem, failure, negative consequence or unfortunate happening, something you'll have to overcome, or what's at stake for the company. The value comes when it's apparent that you have done your homework in coming up with a solution, or the best way for your organization or team to move forward. You express that solution on the heels of expressing the problem.

This is more likely to get people on board and supportive of you. You use your emotion to express the importance of the issue, the importance of the greater good, the possibilities, and the solution. In other words, you rally people with your emotion instead of dragging them down.

I was so moved by my influencer's response to me that day that I did two things:

1.   I looked back and realized that any time I had been passionate and emoted in this way, it worked. This was a big aha moment.

2. I decided to deliberately start emoting whenev-
    er I could, with my staff, board, colleagues, and
    stakeholders. I may need to govern my emotions
    or purge them if they're negative, but no more
    tamping them down.

Why does this work?

Because when you emote about a problem and focus on its solution, articulating everyone's role in it, you show leadership. And people want leadership, particularly when they are facing a challenge or crisis.

I learned that day that emoting to solve a problem is seen as positive, even though the problem itself is negative. You can even articulate how negative the problem is—meaning the negative impact it is having on the team or the organization and the greater good it stands in the way of.

Once the negative consequence is expressed, however, you must quickly pivot, and turn to the solution. The key is to emote with a giving mindset to add value and direction. You can be honest (as long as it's respectful and appropriate), but your emoting must lead toward something positive—not complaining, being a victim, or criticizing. Yes, this does mean you have to think through solutions before you express your emotion. It also means you may need to vent with a trusted ally before you go public.

Venting and purging is a good thing. It helps us think more clearly. It helps us go through the grieving process. But this must absolutely be done with a trusted confidant and not with people at work. Having someone you can do this purging and venting with is integral to your success. I'm not telling you not to have negative emotion. I'm just telling you that there is an appropriate time and place to express it. Doing so will renew your spirit to a point so you can focus on the forward momentum when it counts. In my example, I'd had a few weeks to vent with trusted mentors, think through solutions to a significant problem, and refocus.

Of course, I recognize that it's not always possible to step out of a situation to process our emotions. Sometimes an altercation ramps up quickly and we find our emotions welling up. Now, I'm not a person who advocates women crying at work. I'm not judging it, but I don't see men doing that, and they're who I'm usually in the running against. Instead, I employ a tool I learned years ago at a seminar that allowed me to dissolve my tears when my emotions are threatening to get the better of me.

Let's say someone yells at you at work—which is completely inappropriate, by the way—and you feel the tears welling up in your eyes. Just tell yourself, in your mind, to *stop*. Slowly tilt your head back, almost like you are giving the words you just heard some thought, until you are looking at the ceiling. Now, blink your eyes gently a few times. This causes the tears to recede back into your head. Take a deep breath while you are there, and when the tears fully dissipate, which only takes a few seconds, slowly tilt your head back to normal and look at your assailant. Then you can say something really great, like, "I'm going to take what you said and think about it. Thank you for your feedback. I'll get back to you," and, if you can, walk away. Give yourself the time and distance you need to recover from the attack.

I realize that you will not be able to walk away every time.

But you will be able to tilt your head back and get those tears dissipated, and this works in your favor. When this happened to me, the assailant later said, "You scared me when you did that. I thought you were going to deck me!" I had to laugh, but the point is, it takes the person off guard and they don't know what to think. When things get heated, it is definitely about who has the emotional upper hand. This tactic not only dissolves our tears, but can sometimes make the person standing in front of you rally a little respect. And that's what we need, right?

Sometimes we have to discern exactly what we are getting emotional about. Think of someone who gives you legitimate feedback but with a very nasty and harsh delivery. You may get emotional about the delivery, causing you to discount the feedback. That's dangerous for you because the feedback may be valuable or even vital to your success. So, take some time to separate the emotion from the message and vent where you need to: behind the scenes. Then go back and address the feedback, absent of the emotion, and evaluate it honestly. Once you do that, you'll be able to look at a strategy to address it going forward.

Just remember that when you emote, you should do so with a mission to strive for the greater good of the organization, and with a giving mindset. This is why our definition of emoting includes the words "forward momentum." That is the key difference between welcome and unwelcome emotions.

To make it easy for you, here's a chart of the dos and don'ts of emoting in the workplace:

Dos	**Don'ts**
Honest/genuine	Hostile/angry
Solution-oriented	Victim-focused
Forward-looking	Complaining
Encouraging	Downer
Focus on situation	Focus on the personal
(Respond)	(React)

Note that the "Do" column has positive and forward-leaning adjectives that involve responding to a situation, whereas the "Don't" column has negative and backward-leaning characteristics that are often felt when we react to a situation. To be successful leaders, we have to be in the respond mode more than the react mode. And that's the major difference.

Once you can place your emotions into either one of these columns, it becomes easy to see which will serve you or hurt you in the workplace. When a hurtful emotion arises, you'll know you need to process that emotion outside the work environment so you can strategize your response to the situation. So, make it simple and use this chart to ask yourself, is this emotion one that is going to serve me (respond to the situation) or hurt me (react to the situation)?

There is another way to leverage emoting to build your influence. If you adopt this strategy, you will add jet fuel to your influencing skills.

Here's what you do: add the habit of "serial emoting" as a daily and ongoing habit. What I mean by this is to enthusiastically recognize people around you on a daily basis. Casually recognizing people on the fly allows you to build your positive emoting skills and reputation as a leader. This means developing the habit of smaller gestures that bring connection and joy to people, but don't take you a lot of time. Think of them as sincere, random acts of verbal kindness.

Here are some ways you can serially emote:

1. Notice others' successes
2. Compliment others (be genuine)
3. Notice the good in others
4. Thank people
5. Recognize positive change
6. Connect others to a higher purpose (company mission)
7. Inspire others

Just like giving, you can emote casually and enthusiastically to increase your influence. You can also emote by celebrating others publicly. Call out the good things they are doing or recognize their contributions. Tie in your values and goals, or the greater good as to why it's important, and you will intensify your impact. Here's an example, taken from an email I wrote to a former boss after an event we hosted.

"Great remarks at the podium tonight. I love how you tied our mission (to serve the public servant) to our program. You really captured the hearts of our audience. Thank you for your leadership."

Not only did I acknowledge his success, but I tied it to our mission and our ability to influence our members. Also note that I used a word rarely heard in the workplace: love. When you look at all that is going on in the world today, is there any doubt in your mind that we need more love everywhere? Be the one to fill that void.

Make it your goal to become a serial "complimenter"—you know, the type of person who always sees the good in others and expresses it. You can do this with your everyday acquaintances, your fellow employees, your influencers, and your peers. You never know who will give you a leg up when you need it, so make serial complimenting a broad habit.

You can emote about their accomplishments (large and small); their talents; their tenacity in getting a job done; their commitment or passion; the report they gave; a presentation they did well; or their approach to some project. By helping others feel their goodness, you will feed their soul and build your own influence and power at the same time. People LOVE to be recognized with sincerity and enthusiasm. Give that emotion broadly and watch your influence grow. It feels good, and it's good for you!

The reason it's so good for you is that positivity is contagious, and an attitude of gratitude is always the mindset of a leader. So allow your serial emoting to become a feeder of your heart's gratitude for people. Everyone has something to offer, so figure out what each brings to the table and recognize it, and cultivate that gratitude within yourself.

Use emoting to build as many positive relationships as you can. You don't need to devote a lot of time to it. Emote where you can and when appropriate so that you are recognized as someone with positive influence at all levels.

I have a mentor who says, "America is emotionally flat-lining." It's true! Many work environments are monotone, homogenized, vanilla. And yet people want deeper meaning. With focus and vision, you can elevate the emotional flatliners, bring them to a higher level, and identify yourself as a leader.

People are starved for deeper meaning; they are starved for someone to connect today to a better tomorrow, to connect what we do every day with a grander purpose. They want to be recognized for the good they bring to the table. Be the person to give that to them.

This emoting skill is innate within us as woman, yet we are often told to tamp down or restrain ourselves. That's wrong, and to do so you would be wasting one of our greatest assets. You don't need to tamp down your emotion—you just need to channel it, govern it effectively, and use your strength for good.

Emoting is energy. When it is forward-moving and focused on strengths, solutions, and opportunities, is massively positive. When it is looking backward, at mistakes, bad deeds, or problems (with no solution), it's massively negative. And that's why complainers and those who are always pointing out problems with nothing positive to say or any solutions are not seen as leaders, but as a drag on the organization.

Now I'm not saying to placate others. That lacks integrity. I'm saying find the true assets in others, be a problem-solver, and emote in large and small situations with positive emotion. Use your power of emoting for good.

Earlier I mentioned the use of the word "love." After my successful experience emoting at the board meeting, I decid-ed to experiment with using the word love more often in the workplace. I decided to start saying, "Love you!" when certain people left our office after meetings. Of course, I was careful who I said this to. I didn't want to be misunderstood or offend anyone, or worse, get sued. But I also wanted to add a deeper sense of comradery to our workplace. And I succeeded in that.

Note that, just like the strategy I shared about referring to older men as "young man," you have to have a strong rapport and mutual trust with people, as well as have found a successful way of bantering to get away with this. When I first started saying, "Love You" at work, members of my team were taken aback. They didn't say anything, but I could see it in their faces. Over time, the shock changed to softness. I even noticed some of the most stoic and surly men leaving our office with a lighthearted "Love you, too!"

Now, I want to be clear that I am not suggesting you go to work tomorrow and start saying, "love you." You have to interact with people in ways they are comfortable with, so you put them at ease. And this requires some discernment of what is appropriate for the situation.

My situation was unique because of the intense nature of working in a nonprofit with politics as the backdrop. People and organizations were often used as political footballs, being kicked around and attacked with lies, deceit, and false press. These unfortunate and harsh tactics have a negative impact on the morale of people and organizations. The relationships that develop between individuals on the same side of this battlefield who are trying to prevent the destruction of the good work they do are vastly deeper than the working relationships of the typical workplace. The deep bonds that develop in this heated and extreme situation, the humanity it reveals when the team feels defeated, and the stamina it takes to come together and win is intense. In this situation, "love you" was not such a stretch as it would have been in other types of businesses and work environments. It was an equal counterbalance to the barrage of negativity and inhumanity that we would often endure day to day. That's why it was such a game-changer in my situation. When we felt beat up by our environment, we knew we had each other, and the light-hearted expression of love (platonic love) pulled us up by our bootstraps and let us know we could lean on each other.

So, my point in sharing this with you is not to suggest you start staying "love you" at work, but to show you how powerful and contagious positive emoting can be. It can literally pull someone out of a depressed state. Positive emoting, whether it's using the word love or passionately discussing the solution to a problem, has a huge impact on the building of positive relationships at work and on your own psychology, and it builds your brand as a leader.

It has been proven that successful people think positive thoughts more often than unsuccessful people. So use your ability to positively emote frequently to share positive sentiments and watch your influence grow. People will be drawn to you.

Here are some more examples of things I've said to colleagues "on the fly" in my own serial emoting efforts.

"Hey Jim, you always hold the door open for me and I think that's so nice! What a gentleman you are!"

"Jesse, I saw the report you did. Great job! The way

you convey your ideas makes a complex subject very easy to understand."

"Hey Stacy. I love how you just put that customer's mind at ease. I'm going to take a lesson from your approach. Thanks!"

Start looking for the large and small positives about everyone around you and emote about it. When I did this, my world started changing—I fostered better relationships, and found more people were willing to go to bat for me.

When I left my career in the public policy nonprofit, the impact of my emoting was summarized by one female elected official who said, "People are drawn to you. We'll miss you."

This touched me deeply, and it demonstrated that my strategy for emoting had worked beyond my expectations.

So, be that woman people are drawn to. Give them deeper meaning. Emote with positive thought and vision behind it—to solve problems and recognize other's strengths—and you will find yourself being viewed as a leader.

So, to recap, in this chapter we learned the most and least effective ways to use your emoting. We learned that we can express emotions about a negative consequence or outcome, as long as we quickly pivot to talking about solutions with forward momentum. We learned to focus on responding to situations, rather than reacting.

We learned how to purge unwanted emotions outside the work environment so we can get to a productive place emotionally, and that to do so we must have a trusted confidant outside the workplace. We also discussed why emoting is important to human beings in general, and encouraged you to become a serial emoter so you can connect those around you to a higher purpose.

Now we're ready to move on to Chapter 3, Leveraging.

"Fair play doesn't pertain in bargaining.
What matters there is leverage."
~ Alan Rosenberg

Chapter 3
Leveraging

I n this chapter, I'm going to show you how leveraging is a strength that is both vital and natural to you. I'll also walk you through leveraging your influencers in order to advance, including when it's appropriate and how to make the ask. Lastly, I'll show you how to use leveraging to build community around those you want to influence.

The definition of leveraging, for our purposes, is:

> *Utilizing a person, group or situation to influence an outcome that could not be achieved on your own.*

Leveraging is an interesting word. For some, it conjures up images of shady backroom deals. Others envision a businessman standing firm in a bold black suit and squinting into a camera lens for the cover shot of Money Magazine. These are stereotypes. The fact is, most women spent their lives artfully leveraging, often without even realizing it. It's an innate strength that we have.

The concept of leveraging for influence is actually pretty simple. Leveraging is using Borrowed Influence (remember, this is the influence of title, position, or status; in this case, the title position or status of an influencer) to help you achieve a goal. If you have ever asked someone else to do something for you because you thought they would get a more positive response than you, then you have leveraged. It's not bad. It's smart. Let me give you some examples that might sound familiar...

- When you were little, did you ever ask a friend to ask your mom if they could stay for dinner, because you thought if you asked yourself, Mom would say no? (That's leveraging.)
- As a kid, did you ever go to one parent over another with a request, because you thought that parent was more likely to say yes, then would bring the other parent along for the ride? (That's leveraging.)
- As a parent, did you ever ask your child to ask your spouse for something, like going out to dinner? You know your spouse doesn't want to go, so instead of asking yourself, you have your child ask because your spouse would have a harder time saying no to them. (That's leveraging.)
- Or, have you ever asked a friend or colleague to make a request of someone, because you know they are more likely to get a favorable response than you are? (That's leveraging.)

Basically, if you have ever asked anyone to "do your bidding for you" you have leveraged. Let's face it—we have this skill nailed, ladies. Now it's time to use it in a professional setting because unless we do we will never be as successful as our male counterparts. Here's why leveraging is such a vital strength in business:

Whether you like it or not, not everyone will like you. It's just a fact. Not everyone you need will be on your side. As much as we'd like that, it's just not reality.

Ask yourself, do you like everyone? Probably not. So why do we have the unrealistic expectation that everyone will like us? If we understand this and accept it, we can clearly see why leveraging is a necessary female strength that we need to be utilizing. How on earth could we possibly progress without it?

When I started my nonprofit, I knew there were people who would tell me no. To get the critical mass I needed, I leveraged. And you can use this natural female strength as well.

This is where you get a return on the work you did to build solid relationships with your influencers. You gave to them, and at some point the relationship became strong enough that they want to give back.

This is why I advised you in the beginning to read through the entire book before implementing these strategies. Once you understand the skill of leveraging, you'll be better able to discern which influencers are likely to support you. Those who are not willing to support, help, or sponsor you are not leverageable, so you don't have to waste your valuable time trying to build a relationship with them. In fact, these are the people you'll have to use leverage ON if you need their support.

What do I mean by this? When you know (or become aware) that someone is a roadblock (will not support you, despite your best relationship building efforts), you'll likely want to drop them off your influencer list. That said, you may at some point still need their support, or at minimum need them NOT to work against you. If this is the case, look at their network of connections and relationships and find someone with whom they have a strong relationship, then build a relationship with that person. Later, you may be able to leverage their influence to overcome your roadblock.

Leveraging starts with relationships. When I built the relationships that I would later lean on to get votes and start my organization, I really had no idea how I'd leverage them. I was just focused on my immediate goal, which was to get them to know and value me now so they would help me expand my organization later. And, after I had been giving to them for some time, that's what eventually happened. They got to see my vision and strategy, thoughts and ideas, and I was able to leverage them effectively in a crisis.

As you've probably surmised by now, you can only leverage a seasoned relationship with your influencer. If you're not sure whether your relationship has seasoned, ask yourself the following: "Has this relationship blossomed into a give-give relationship?"; "Have I learned all I can about my influencer and given so much that they have started to get to know me and my goals and aspirations?"; "Have they indicated a willingness to help me in any way?"; "Have they made any small, supportive gestures that indicate they might be ready to be asked for more substantial support without feeling used?"; "Have they started reciprocating my giving in any way?" If the answer is yes to any of these questions, your relationship is starting to season.

How long does it take to build a seasoned, give-give relationship? It's different for everyone. Some can take a few months; some can take years. Sometimes it depends on how your influencer views relationships; other times it may depend on how big your ask is. You might be able to ask for something small relatively quickly, but for the big asks that involve some risk, you'd better have a highly matured relationship. You'll likely know when you have the type of relationship that you can lean on. And if you're not sure, test the waters in small ways and observe the response.

Once you've developed some semblance of a reliable give-give relationship, look for opportunities to open up about your ideas, goals, and objectives. Be cautious at first—don't go all in. Tiptoe gingerly and see what the response is. The idea is to start making them aware of your talent, your enthusiasm, your quality as a professional and, ultimately, your goal. You want them to care so much about you and your goal that you are able to coopt them to help you reach it.

As you talk to your influencer about your goals, your skills, successes, and accomplishments, watch how they react. Pay attention when they "perk up" about something you say and listen attentively to their responses and advice.

You also might ask them for their feedback on how to meet your goal. As I discussed in the chapter on giving, utilizing your influencer as a mentor is a great strategy when building your relationship. Most people love giving advice and are flattered when they are seen as the go-to expert. This type of exchange also gives you the opportunity to share more about your own expertise, accomplishments, vision, and aspirations. It is also part of the "seasoning" process that brings you closer to be able to leverage your influencer in some way.

Now, let's move on to some ways that you can leverage your influencer. The list below is by no means exhaustive, but it will give you an idea of how incredibly beneficial these relationships can be.

1. Utilize them to create "eye-opening" moments with other influencers or roadblocks (sometimes just being seen with them can help)
2. As a reference for a job opportunity
3. To help you get a job opportunity
4. To elevate your status/credibility/respect with others
5. To get introductions/meet other influencers
6. To shorten your path to your goal (mentoring)
7. To lend credibility to an idea you have
8. To present your idea
9. To get feedback to make your idea more "sell-able"
10. To gain insider information (players, organizational politics, culture)
11. To devise a roadmap to your goal (strategy)
12. To help you surround others with community (more on this later)
13. To give you advice
14. To be a sounding board for direction or in a crisis
15. To make a request on your behalf, or instead of you
16. To advocate for you or your idea
17. To lead or support a project or idea you have
18. To participate in a group or committee that you lead, or that is related to your goal

Another way is to leverage your relationship to gain access

to another influencer who is currently "untouchable" to you. Oftentimes your influencer can open doors or even pave the way with a preliminary conversation. You might ask your influencer about the best way to approach someone, and they may then offer to help.

Your influencer may also neutralize "roadblocks"—those people who are either ambivalent toward you or completely against you. This works when your influencer is a trusted and needed ally of your roadblock. The roadblock needs your influencer as much as you do, so they end up supporting you too because they want to maintain the lifeline relationship they have with your influencer.

You want to be careful when leveraging your influencer to help you with a roadblock. Proceed with caution. You don't want to make negative statements about your roadblock, but rather approach the conversation gracefully. When dealing with a roadblock, you'll want to think through the best way to neutralize them. It may not be a matter of your influencer having a direct conversation with them. Perhaps your strategy entails surrounding your "roadblock" with a community of like-minded individuals, so that they become the "odd man out" if they don't support you. We'll discuss how to surround people with community in a bit.

Most influencers will help you in some way, especially if you've given to them and supported them and built a strong, give-give relationship.

As you can see, there are a number of ways to leverage an influencer relationship. Spend some time thinking about it and make a list for each of your influencers on the things they can do that would be most valuable for you. Then strategize the best way to approach the conversation. I strongly advise having a coach in this work. People can be complicated, especially influencers, so making sure you deliver your ask in the right way can increase the likelihood of a yes answer.

Another way to leverage is to surround people with a like-minded community that influences them to get on board. How many times have you been in a meeting and seen consensus grow because a number of people expressed support? What you'll find is that the larger the number of people that express support, the more support the idea will get from others around the same table.

Why does this work? Because people are largely risk-averse. They want to go with strength, with something that already appears successful. They want to go with a winner. When you reach critical mass around a meeting table, other people around the table see that as strength, so they pile on.

Before surrounding someone with a likeminded community, you first have to do some legwork to create a community that will actually rally. This means approaching influencers and potentially other meeting participants beforehand—with a phone call or even face-to-face.

The "meeting before the meeting" is an area in which women can take a page from the male playbook. This is a behavioral dynamic that has been fully revealed by author and trainer, Pat Heim, author of *Hardball for Women*. Women think the meeting is to discuss and decide. Men typically go to the meeting with their minds made up because they've already discussed the topic (oftentimes on the golf course or at happy hour) and come to a conclusion. For them, the meeting is not to discuss and decide. It's to confirm what they've already decided. This is not devious; it's actually quite brilliant. And all you have to do is understand this and do the same thing. In my nonprofit career, I had a rule: "Never go into a meeting without knowing what the outcome is going to be." I made this happen with community-building via phone calls, meetings, and requests beforehand.

You may say, "This isn't right. The meeting is for us to debate and decide," and if everyone on the team thought and behaved that way, it would be fine. As I shared before, however, men are often playing a different game, so if you start to realize that decisions are being confirmed at meetings rather than made, you may have the "meeting before the meeting" dynamic happening in your workplace.

Now it's time for you to play by the same rules. Have your meeting before the meeting to cultivate support and build the community that will surround your roadblocks when it counts.

When strategizing around this I highly recommend working with a coach or consultant who knows how to do this type of influencing. You might also ask one of your influencers to be your sounding board while you discuss this strategy. Know that this is an advanced skill. I don't want you to get into trouble here. As I've been saying throughout the book, start gingerly and note the outcome. Proceed with caution, but definitely proceed. This is a strategy in your toolbox that will serve you well. Learn to use it.

Here's an example from my own coaching practice on surrounding people with community. Three young women approached me at one of my speaking events. They were tired of going to staff meetings where male colleagues bragged about their accomplishments and they could not get a word in edgewise. They said it wasn't so much about the men's bragging as it was the fact that the women felt they were actually running circles around the men and not being recognized for it. The problem was, the women were so humble, using words like "we" and "us" instead of "I," and were often talked over and interrupted at the meetings. The result was that their accomplishments were being overlooked by the boss.

In speaking to these women I also learned that they had a hard time speaking up about their own accomplishments. After I coached them on how to do this, they met with each other before the next staff meeting to discuss what they were doing and what they had recently achieved. Then, they all agreed to recognize each other for these accomplishments at the next meeting. If one of them got cut off, another one would chime in and reiterate the recognition of the other. Sure enough, by the time that staff meeting was over they'd all recognized each other for their significant weekly accomplishments—and made the boss aware of their good work.

This meeting was the beginning of a shift in the workplace dynamic. The women became more comfortable talking about their achievements, and the boss started to realize how much value they brought to the table. Eventually, he even started asking for specific reports from each woman—all because these women leveraged each other in staff meetings, and surrounded their boss with community of support. They built up the recognition of their hard work and made their accomplishments known and valued.

Here's a recap of how to have the "meeting before the meeting":

1. Meet with the right people before the meeting
2. Get feedback and massage the idea ahead of time
3. Preplan the outcome you want and get buy-in
4. Plan a talking order that builds support (advanced)
5. Plan specific comments around the table (advanced)
6. Attain your desired outcome by surrounding people with community

In this chapter we learned what real leveraging is. We learned how the vital strength of leveraging is natural to you. We learned how to leverage your influencers to advance, including when it's appropriate to make the ask. Lastly, we learned how to use leverage through building community around those we want to influence in groups. We also suggested getting a coach, consultant, or influencer to help you strategize when you start to employ the strategy of surrounding people with community, because it's an advanced skill and requires some finesse.

Leveraging is a strength that is typically attributed to men. But think about all of the innate female abilities it takes to leverage, namely, problem-solving, creativity, intuition, collaboration, bridge-building, dot-connecting, resourcefulness, and compromise. These skills are in our female DNA. Don't feel guilty about leveraging. Use your power for good, and leverage to succeed.

To help you deepen your understanding of ways to leverage,

here are a few case studies.

Case Study 1
Overcoming Unconscious Bias

One of the best working relationships I've ever developed is so solid that he became a family friend, yet he still has a hard time seeing my wisdom sometimes. I don't know what it is about men, but sometimes they just cannot accept the package the information is coming in—in this case, the packaging of a woman. As in this instance, once in a while, one of my influencers would become a roadblock, and I would have to leverage another influencer with them.

On this particular occasion, I could clearly see that my friend/influencer/roadblock would have valued the idea if a man was presenting it. While this was frustrating, I didn't blame him for this bias. This man had supported me so much I knew his bias had to be unconscious. So, I went about my strategy to engage another influencer (one that he respected) to get support for the idea.

I knew of several men he respected, including one I was particularly close with because he worked for me as a consultant. I approached him privately with the idea, and he loved it; in fact, he even added some value to it (which is exactly what we should be getting from our influencers). I asked for his support in pitching it to my roadblock. We had a lot of trust between us, so I was able to be forthright with him about the situation without jeopardizing myself. I then planned a lunch with the three of us, and asked my consultant to broach the subject while I remained quiet. You see, we had agreed beforehand that the idea needed to come off just a little different from the one I'd already pitched. We also took the time to connect the idea to something my influencer-turned-roadblock valued.

We had the lunch and it went smoothly. I got the support I wanted. At the end of the meeting, I was surprised when my influencer-turned-roadblock-turned-influencer turned to me and said, "This was a lot like your prior idea, but I think it's better. I liked how (consultant's name here) suggested we approach it." I laughed to myself because the new approach was exactly what my consultant and I had discussed as we planned for the meeting. It had worked out perfectly.

Case Study 2
Building Strength Around a Board Table

One of the things that really made me understand the importance of having the "meeting before the meeting" and surrounding people with community was an incident that happened at one of my board meetings.

A female board member had brought up a great idea at the meeting. Unfortunately, she had not done her homework. She didn't realize how this worked and was expecting people to love her idea and spontaneously hop on board. This was risky on her part.

Instead of consensus, she got only one other board member (out of twenty-four) to speak up in support of the idea. Everyone else was silent. It felt like they wanted to think about it more, even though nobody was saying that.

Then, out of nowhere, another board member started talking negatively about the idea, followed by another, who piled on with his negative comments. Within minutes, two others sounded off about the idea's lack of merit, and I could clearly see sentiment around the table starting to shift toward disapproval. Once that critical mass had been reached, people around the table followed.

Like I said, people are risk-averse. They want to go with strength. Unfortunately, the strength around the table had grown in the negative direction once four people had voiced their concerns. The number of negative comments had hit critical mass, and the balance tipped against her.

If only she'd had the meetings she needed to have before the meeting, massaged the idea with the feedback she received, planned some comments around the table, and then presented it, she would have likely gotten the support she was after. Instead, the idea got a no vote that day, which meant it was not coming back up in the future. A good idea died for lack of behind-the-scenes preparation, and this board member didn't even know what hit her.

Case Study 3
Stealing Your Ideas

Theft of your ideas is one of the most irritating things that can happen in your career. It has happened to me; in fact, I can recall a couple of people who regularly stole things I said and program ideas I had. This was not only petty, but frustrating, because I was trying to build my brand as a valuable professional.

So, I adopted a strategy. I started sharing my ideas with influencers and other select people before I ever went public with the idea or shared it in a meeting. This way, if one of these thieves tried to take it, people would already know where it had come from. Just as important, I made sure my ideas were very well developed and in the planning phases before any announcements were made. We'd get it going in a significant way, all under the radar. By the time it went public, or was divulged in a meeting, the project was in process or near completion. No one could steal it, because it had already been done.

It was unfortunate to have to do this, but it was preferable to the alternatives—allowing the theft of my ideas to continue and/or complaining about it—neither of which is the mark of a leader. To progress and reach my goals, the right people had to know how creative and visionary I could be, and this strategy, a form of leveraging, served me well.

Case Study 4
Trust Capital

When you conduct your career by leveraging your 5 innate female strengths, you will, at some point, have accumulated your own amount of influence—both borrowed and earned. When this happens, people will come to you asking for favors, one of which will be an introduction to one of your influencers. You know, those relationships you invested hours, days, and years building to help you advance your career? Yeah, they want access to that.

One thing I learned the hard way is that when we work this hard to build influencer relationships, we also build up trust capital. What this means is that we have a certain amount of clout with the influencer, similar to the "love bank" or "trust bank" we discussed earlier. That clout is a valuable commodity and not to be taken lightly. When you refer someone to an influencer that they would not otherwise have access to, you risk expending some of your trust capital with this influencer. Therefore, you must ask yourself if this person will be responsible and respectful with your referral? Will they treat your influencer the way they should?

I recall the time a close associate asked me to open a door with an influencer. I wanted to help, so I said yes; I also had to do some groundwork to help my influencer understand why he should take the meeting, and what I was hoping it would do for him. I was already taking up his valuable time by talking about someone else's priorities.

I got the meeting all set up, then guess what? The requestor didn't show up to the meeting. When I called them on it, they responded by acting as though it was no big deal and that they had decided to go in a different direction.

As you can imagine, I was now in for a very uncomfortable conversation, one in which I had to tell my influencer that this person had changed their mind, implying that my contact didn't think highly enough of him, or me, to even make a phone call. It made me look bad and like an inept judge of character. It made me look like I was wasting my influencer's time. And it made me look less sophisticated than I wanted my influencer to see me. It was a hard lesson.

Keep your influencer relationships close. Only connect people to them once they have done their work (i.e. through giving) to build a trusting relationship with you. Don't risk the precious trust capital you have worked so hard to build on someone who may not understand or respect the value of influencer relationships. Just decline.

Case Study 5
Board Membership

After I'd launched my new nonprofit, I started the effort of building it into a more robustly influential organization. To do that, I needed the majority of influential organizations in the area to be represented on my board. I was able to entice many of them with a mere explanation of our mission, and leveraged their desire to be "at the table" with local policy decision-makers. It worked.

I was aware of a couple roadblocks who would tell me no, and I needed their organizations to be members and lend their influence to our board. After some strategizing, I decided not to ask them to join myself and instead found two people who were influential to my roadblocks and had them make the ask.

The first influencer was easy, because he was my president. He wanted the organization to be influential and since he was a public figure, my roadblocks needed him. He was perfect. He was also very close with a couple of other influencers and thought he could bring them along by leveraging the elevated status it would bring to them as leaders. So, they went off to meet with my roadblocks, asking them to join our organization and sit on our board. I was far away from those meetings. After one of them, I got a phone call from my president saying, "Guess who our newest member is?" We had success twice with this approach. I had now secured my target organizations on my board by leveraging a few people that my roadblocks needed, valued, and wanted to please.

Now let's move on to your fourth innate female strength, Delivering.

*"This struggle is real. The juggle is real.
That's why everyone should hire working mothers.
They are put in crazy situations all the time
and are forced to problem-solve.
They are some of my most resourceful employees."
~ Sara Blakely*

Chapter 4
Delivering

N one of your strengths matter unless you can deliver. The definition of delivering, for our purposes, is:

Bringing value, results, and outcomes to fruition that your stakeholders value

Delivering successfully involves your ability to provide value and desired outcomes to the people who matter—influencers who can have an impact on your future. The good news is, women are hardwired to deliver.

Have you ever heard the comment, "If you want to get something done, give it to a woman?" Everyone knows women excel in this area. We have the innate ability to figure out how to "do it all." Perhaps it's because we have historically borne a disproportionate burden of family relationships, raising children, and maintaining the general peace and pace in our family circles. Though the reason is not exactly clear, it is increasingly recognized, even by men, that we can be far more capable than they are in this regard.

Take, for example, the discovery made by Kevin O'Leary, the billionaire who became a household name from his mainstay appearances on the show *Shark Tank*. On *Shark Tank*, investors hear pitches from entrepreneurs who request funding for their businesses. Sharks invest if they think a company can turn a profit and make them money.

A few years ago Kevin O'Leary asked his staff to investigate what his most profitable companies have in common. Do you know what they discovered? They were all run by women!

Later, his team went back and investigated what the women were doing differently from their male counterparts. They found distinctly different approaches to business in three key areas.

1. The women were more likely to reach their goals. The women set more realistic and pragmatic goals and often met or exceeded them at the end of the year. (The men's goals were often loftier and not met as often.)

2. The women had happier teams. There were two reasons for this.

    a. The women showed more compassion and collaborative leadership styles than the men, making their employees happier.
    b. The employees were also happier because their company was reaching their goals. It was a rewarding place to work because they could see the success they were creating.

3. The women prioritized better. Specifically, they found that women who were moms were better at prioritizing at work because they were used to having to juggle their careers and family. They utilized their limited time more efficiently, which meant their companies and teams were more likely to focus on the most important things, making them more productive and more successful.

For so long it was a negative in the workforce to be a mother; we had to downplay our commitment to our families in order to be viewed as someone who could carry the weight of a significant professional job.

Who would have ever thought that would shift—that the skills employed by mothers would be recognized as assets in the workplace? I got tears in my eyes when I heard that one. It's about time! Now we just need Kevin O'Leary and others to spread the word to employers. I've been doing my part by really honing in on this in my recent talks because it can be such a gamechanger for women.

Now that we know you can deliver profit, often better than the guys, let's talk about who decides if you are delivering successfully, namely, your employer, your customers, your partners, and your influencers. This is why it's so important to think of yourself as your own company. Because delivering requires holding yourself accountable to results that bring value to those you serve.

In this work of delivering value, it's easy to get bogged down. While we are good at focusing on only the most important things, it's also true that we can get in a mode of overdelivering, just like we can get in the mode of over-giving. For this reason, I have to address the idea of saying no. Knowing when to say no is an important skill, but it's one that some women struggle with. So let me give you a simple and quick strategy for determining what you should say no to.

First, you have to know your priorities. Write down your top three or four priorities in order of importance. I share mine below so you have an example.

1. My faith
2. My husband/family
3. Making money
4. Helping other people reach their goals

The priorities you come up with should be the priorities for your entire life, not just your work environment. In order to be truly successful, you have to be a happy person and nobody is happy while they are ignoring their personal life. In reality, you only have one life, so determine your priorities for that one life.

You'll notice that my number one is my faith. I know I need to get my head straight first thing in the morning or the day will likely not be as good as it could or should be. So I make it a point each morning to get in touch with my values, beliefs, and faith so that the foundation I'm operating from is always solid.

Next comes my husband and family. I put my husband first because I believe that the family is not successful unless the marriage unit leading it is in good shape. Again, I'm concentrating on a strong foundation.

Next comes making money. Money comes before my mission because I have to have income in order to maintain my ability to focus on my top two priorities, which are my faith and my husband and family.

This leads to my fourth priority, my mission for my life, which is helping others and groups of people reach their goals.

Some people might say that because I listed faith and family as my first and second priorities, I am not truly dedicated to my career. That's not true. In fact, my career is supported most effectively when I am healthy in the areas of faith and family. Faith and family are the necessary foundation for me to experience any success at all.

And, just because faith and family are numbers one and two doesn't mean they get most of my time. They don't. In fact I actually spend most of my waking hours on priorities three and four. So you see, this list doesn't dictate my how much time each gets on my schedule. What this list does do is help me answer three very important questions when I cannot or don't want to do it all.

When you cannot do it all, or want to decide if you should be taking on a project or task, get your priorities in order and ask yourself these three questions.

1. Does this task or project align with any of my priorities? [If it doesn't, dump it and never think about it again. If it does, go on to question two.]

2. Is this task or project taking away something sig-nificant from one of my higher priorities? [This is a vital question because only you can determine what significant means. Suffice it to say, if the cost of doing the task or project creates signifi-cantly negative impacts on a higher priority it's likely best to let it go.) If it doesn't, or the impact to the higher priority is temporary and you are okay with that, move on to question three.]

3. Does this task or project significantly move me toward my goal(s)? (Remember, you identified your goals in Chapter 1.) If the task or project in question does not have the potential to move you significantly toward one of your goals (either immediately or over time), it's probably okay to

dump it.

You may have a lot of opportunities coming your way that seem appealing. They may seem like the right thing to do. They may be compelling, enriching, and even fun. But if they don't move your life in the direction you want it to go, then they are actually doing more harm than good.

I'm not saying this is always an easy process to go through. Sometimes the answers to these questions get complex, with tradeoffs being made here and there. That's fine. You can recalibrate if need be. But if you don't go through a prioritizing process, you may find yourself taking on unnecessary projects and be stunted, if not derailed from reaching your goals. Delivering does not mean doing it all. It means doing all that is necessary to reach your goals. And to do that, you need written goals, a priority list, and the answers to the three questions above.

Even after prioritizing you may find that you still have a lot on your plate, and that's normal. If you are reading this book, you are probably a high-performer and hold yourself to a high production standard. If after using this process you need another tool to help you further prioritize I would highly recommend the Eisenhower Matrix.

The Eisenhower Matrix is simple. President Dwight D. Eisenhower used it every day to decide what to spend his time on when he was running our country. It's brilliant and I think will be eye-opening for you. We are not going to go into detail about the Eisenhower Matrix here, but it's easy to find on the Internet. Use it when you have priorities that make it through the prior process but are still likely to bog you down. Look for a site that not only describes the Eisenhower Matrix but tells you how to use it. You'll find yourself saying no to far more than you thought you could, and you'll be a lot happier.

The last thing I'll share on prioritizing is the concept of "the sprint." Sometimes it makes sense to make a herculean effort that may impinge temporarily on our priorities, in exchange for a big win or advancement toward our goals.

For instance, my husband decided to get his bachelor's degree at fifty-nine years old. This was a time commitment much more significant than we would typically accept of a project; however, we saw it as a sprint. In other words, it would cause some pain for a while, but would not be a permanent way of life. It would also eventually add to our way of life and help him reach a big goal on his list. The tradeoff was more than worth it.

You too will have projects and opportunities that are worthy of a "sprint." You may need to discuss it with your family or with your boss, but the temporary pain will be worth it for the gain on the other side.

A mentor of mine regularly reminds me, "Play the game you want to win." I have never wanted a lifestyle in which I'm always working, with no time for myself. Never. In fact, when I allowed myself to work constantly without priorities, thinking that was the key to success, thinking I could do it all, guess what happened. I ignored my personal values, my relationships suffered, and I got sick.

Nobody can function at their highest potential when they are burned out, torn in many directions, have no personal life, and are exhausted. I learned the hard way that I will never feel truly wealthy without my mental and physical health, and without a great family life, so why let them suffer? Yes, I still have huge goals I want to accomplish, but I focus on balancing them with my other priorities, because that's what makes me happy.

So, play the game you want to win. For me, that means having meditation time every morning before work. I make sure my family time is sufficient for the family life I want, with hubby coming first. Making money supports my top two priorities, and then comes work that I am passionate about. Some days I miss my meditation, but by-and-large, I'm living according to my priorities.

The point is, when you focus on your priorities, you will only be spending your time on what is important to you. Not only does this make you a happier person, it brings success to you more quickly. It's also a great motivator that clears much of the busy work from your schedule.

So, make your priority list and check your tasks and projects against it using the three questions I gave you. If you need to, look up the Eisenhower Matrix for the tasks that remain on your list. You'll be a lot better at delivering when you are spending your time on only the most important things. And say no when the task or project doesn't meet with your priorities and goals. You'll find you more easily reach those goals, and you'll be a lot healthier and happier as well.

It's important to point out, that delivering is often like sausage-making. It can be ugly. It doesn't always go as planned. It doesn't matter if the projects and results we are responsible for are for our employer, our family, or our influencers—if we are professional we are in a constant loop of delivering. To make sure you deliver at the highest level, along the way you have to seek feedback and sometimes make course corrections, refine, retool, and re-launch. You are likely to have to reimagine a number of times to get it right, or to respond to changing circumstances.

Think of the restaurant industry and how they have been impacted by Covid lockdowns. The industry has been nearly devastated; however, some restaurant owners pivoted and got creative. I know of one restaurant that applied for a grant and won it. The grant was to feed health care workers. They used the grant to retool their food preparation process and start delivering meals to health care workers at hospitals. They completely changed their business model to survive and they are still in business to this day. Delivering got ugly. They got creative, retooled, pivoted, and saved their business.

Remember, you are like your own business—"Your Name, Inc." This means that when things go sideways (and they will) you will have to pivot so you can keep on delivering. Most people quit too soon. You have all the skills you need within you to make it through this sometimes laborious process. You're likely to have to deal with disappointments, setbacks, broken promises, missteps, surprises, changes, and failures. There will likely be learning lessons, "aha" moments, five steps forward and three steps back. Stick with it and deliver.

And remember, delivering well is in the eyes of the receiver. Just like when building your influencer relationships, do a lot of listening. This way you'll be able to deliver what people want, value, need, and expect, whether they ask for it directly or indirectly.

Delivering usually involves one of the following three basic areas:

1. Solves a problem or alleviates a pain point
2. Adds value
3. Helps reach a goal

So, when you are listening to your influencers, or your employer, or your customers, listen for their pain points, what problems they are experiencing, a way that they may wish things were easier, or something that adds value. If your project, actions, or results fulfill one or more of those areas, then you are likely on the right track.

I built a thirty-year career based on delivering assistance to individuals and industries so they reach their goals. One of my personal talents is seeing solutions to problems that others don't readily see, so I leveraged that by delivering that vision in a package I knew would resonate with my stakeholders. I was able to do this because I had listened to their needs.

Being a great listener is the best way to utilize your strength of delivering. If your boss has never told you what their expectations are, ask them. If they have never told you what success looks like to them, ask them. If they have never told you what they wish would happen, ask them, and then make it happen. This is how you deliver.

Remember to under-promise and overdeliver. This means making your timeline just a bit longer than you need so, you can deliver early and surprise them. Or, deliver what they are looking for but add a little extra that personalizes it and puts that cherry on top.

When you under-promise and overdeliver, you dazzle people. And when you make this a habit with the right people, you build their trust and confidence in you. You will be adding value in such a way that makes them want to keep you in their lives.

If you cannot deliver what you promise, always go back and explain why. Never be silent when your delivery is late or you end up in a crisis that prevents you from delivering. Being forthright and proactive when things don't go as planned builds trust. Let your employer, boss, and influencers know what went wrong, if you can, and give them your new commitment. Again, under-promise and overdeliver, then surprise them with the early delivery or extras that you add on.

Sometimes you'll deliver and it will be out of sight of the right people. This is where you have to do what men do, and that is talk about your accomplishments and wins. Yes, I mean self-promotion. I actually learned how to do this from a man, and by watching him, I learned how to do it without sounding like I'm bragging.

So, how do you self-promote? You handle it as an update in an email or a quick, face-to-face interaction. I'll share how my male mentor did it with me. For a while, he was a consultant for my nonprofit. He was someone that I leveraged over and over because of his deep and meaningful relationships with many influencers. He was masterful at keeping me up to date and well-informed on all he was doing for me.

He wouldn't come in and say, "Hey, I did this cool thing." He would send an email or pop his head in my office door and say, "Hey, I just wanted to let you know that we just received a $15,000 check from XYZ Company. I took the initiative to meet with them and make sure you got their sponsorship check. I wanted to let you know because I know that you stress out about money. So, you can rest easy tonight knowing you have another $15,000 in the bank."

After he left my office, I would be still for a minute and inevitably realize that it had been the best self-promotion effort I'd ever seen. It was not bragging; it was not selfish. It was couched in a way that really made me feel that he was an amazing quarterback on my team and that I needed him. Brilliant!

I adopted this "update method" and it's worked well for me. It takes some thinking about how you'll present the information in a way that aligns with the receivers' needs and values, but it is well worth the time. Because, as we have learned from men, it's not what you know that gets you promoted. It's who knows your impact, and making them feel that they cannot live without you. And that's one way that your value gets communicated without coming off all puffed up.

The last point I want to make about delivering is that it requires you to be a lifelong learner, and be willing to get outside your comfort zone. Things will continue to change at exponential rates. The only way to keep up and continue to offer relevant value is to continue getting training and coaching to learn new skills, and to get comfortable being uncomfortable. Make it a lifetime commitment. It's lifegiving and keeps you young, relevant, and competitive.

And remember, a lot of people do not deliver. It's amazing to me that this is true, but it is. Set yourself apart, surprise your stakeholders, leverage your natural talent, and be that person others know they can count on. Also, you must be willing to evolve. The companies and organizations that fail often do so because they have not adjusted what they are delivering.

Your delivery model must include ongoing monitoring of your environment. That includes what you learn through your giving and listening efforts. It includes what you learn through your leveraging efforts, and the feedback you get along the way. The need for these strengths doesn't go away once your promotion, business, launch, program, product, project, or position is attained. When you use all of your strengths and deliver, you are building a life skill toolbox that results in a trusted brand that people will be loyal to and support. You are inherently good at it, so go out there and dominate in the area of delivering.

To recap, delivering is an innate female strength. To do so successfully, we must prioritize when there's too much on our plate. Value is in the eye of your stakeholders, so listen carefully to what they need and want. Delivering can also get ugly, and the most successful pivot, stick with it, and find a way to keep delivering. Finally, growth happens outside our comfort zone and that lifelong learning is a key to always being able to deliver.

This brings us to your fifth innate strength, Bouncing Back.

"Character cannot be developed in ease and quiet.
Only through experience of trial and suffering
can the soul be strengthened, ambition inspired,
and success achieved."
~ Helen Keller

Chapter 5
Bouncing Back

One well-documented characteristic of successful people is their ability to bounce back quickly from adversity, mistakes, and setbacks. How many people do you know who have fallen short of their goal and launched a full-blown pity party that included every unfortunate circumstance they ever experienced? When you hear this, you know they have not bounced back from past events. Instead of moving forward, they remain stuck, unable to figure out their next right move.

The definition of bouncing back, for our purposes, is:

Your ability to get back on the horse and ride after a failure, disappointment, or setback.

Bouncing back is a choice; however, I advocate for the grieving process when needed. When we experience a loss, we need to grieve. Sometimes we need to vent, cry, or unload. That's okay. It's cathartic and healing. The issue is how long you remain in that space before you move on.

When you need to bounce back from a crisis or loss, ask yourself:

1. What do I need right now?
2. What went wrong, and what can I learn from it?
3. What is my next right move?

Moving through these questions will you help facilitate your bounce back and get to the other side quicker. Question one is about the grieving process and what you need to make yourself comfortable in the moment. It could be to cry, to vent to a trusted friend, or to go to bed. Whatever you need, give it to yourself.

Then, see what you can learn from what happened. Even if the event is something you had no control over, like the death of a loved one, there's something you can learn that will help you move forward. Look for that lesson, because it makes sense of a sometimes nonsensical world. If the event occurred because of a mistake you made, there is definitely something to learn. Do so and move on.

Sometimes, on the heels of a disaster, it can feel overwhelming to think through a complete bounce back strategy. Keep it simple and just ask yourself what your next right move is. You may need to do this several times. Once the next right move is done, then you can ask yourself again, "Now, what is my next right move?" Taking things one step at a time after a crisis allows you to think more clearly, gives you the strength of being able to focus, and helps prevent the overwhelm.

Women have a built-in resilience that enables them to withstand, endure, and look ahead. Countless women bounce back from abuse, cancer, or dysfunction. In fact, according to the Department of Labor, 57% of our workforce is women, so clearly these struggles are not holding us back from our professional lives. That's because we bounce back quicker.

You may find the following scenario familiar. You meet up with a female relative, friend, or colleague for lunch and to get caught up. She is smiling, she looks great, and she seems to have it all together. She seems happy and bubbly, but as your conversation progresses you find out that she has had some horrible illness or dysfunctional situation like a nasty divorce that she's been dealing with. How many of you remember responding with something like, "I had no idea!" You had no idea because women are resilient. She's sitting across from you smiling when she should be crying. She is bouncing back. She is utilizing her female strength of bouncing back to compose herself and move forward.

Of course, there is no better example than the birthing process. We go through this painful physical trauma, and after expelling an entity the size of a watermelon from our bodies we immediately gaze into our child's eyes with loving adoration. That's bouncing back.

Your resilience, as it turns out, has been scientifically studied and proven to be an innate female strength. According to Andy Scharlach, a UC Berkeley professor and director of its Center for the Advanced Study of Aging Services, women generally retain far more resilience as they age than men. This can affect our biological responses to stress, as well as cardiac and cognitive failure. So, where does this resilience come from?

Scharlach contends that it begins very early in life, often before boys and girls learn to read.

> You become resilient by dealing with small-scale stress-ors that you're able to learn from. Women have many more opportunities to do that in their lives than men do, in part because they have more exposure to the stresses that come from being excluded from the privileges that come automatically to little boys. And that continues

throughout women's lives as they carry different bur-
dens and expectations from men. Women still carry
more child rearing responsibilities. They carry more of
the emotional load in families. The gender biases that
exist either beat you down, or you develop a sense of
yourself and others as being okay.

What he is saying here is that we have experienced mi-
croaggressions all our lives and that has caused us to build
resilience that actually prolongs our lives and gives us more
strength and stamina than our male counterparts. Not exactly
the way I'd prefer to build this strength, but since we have it,
it is incumbent upon us to use it to our advantage, both personally and professionally.

In the course of building relationships, you will likely gain
one or more strong, lifeline relationships. Lifeline relationships
can help you bounce back. They are your sounding board,
and can even help you chart a course out of a mess, utilizing
them to help you bounce back. Lean on one of those influencer
relationships that you built through your giving skill. After all,
support is one of the reasons you have built these influencer
relationships in the first place.

Influencers will likely have wise counsel to offer you. Everyone has been in a mess at some point, even and especially
the highly influential. Their help is a reciprocation and you
deserve it for all the giving you've been doing. If you've really
done your giving strategy well, those lifeline relationships will
be there for you in your time of need.

So, go through the labor pains of birthing your goals and
increasing your influence by delivering and bouncing back,

knowing that the offspring of that pain will be your own success and a life you'll love. Endure and welcome the fruits of
your labor by viewing the process as creative and life-giving,
pain included. Re-commit, re-focus, re-tool, re-imagine and
bounce back. It's in your DNA.

*"It boils down to a simple statement:
Women manage risk better. My bias is clearly
on return of capital and low volatility.
I hate to be biased on a gender basis,
but I have become that way."
~Kevin O'Leary*

Conclusion

Friend, it's been such fun teaching you about just how powerful you are. Let's summarize what we've learned about your 5 innate female strengths:

1. Giving – It is your most important strength to build influential, lifeline relationships. Giving starts the process of receiving.

2. Emoting – Builds your brand as a leader, helps you move people forward and tie them to a higher purpose.

3. Leveraging – You must leverage because everyone won't like or support you. Leveraging gets you past your roadblocks and helps you rally groups of people around an idea.

4. Delivering – You can be counted on to deliver what your stakeholders value and need. Retool, get creative and pivot when things don't go as planned.

5. Bouncing Back – It's essential to your success. It's innate in your abilities. Give yourself what you need, learn, and determine your next right move to bounce back quickly.

When it comes to relationships, these strategies work because, as it turns out, we are all individuals with the same basic human and emotional needs. No matter what type of power barrier you find standing in your way, applying the concepts I've given you will help you increase your influence to overcome those barriers and ascend beyond them.

My last question to you is, are you one of those women who wants to advance, but you think you're not ready? This frustrates me because while the world is waiting for your strengths, men are stepping up, even some that are not fully qualified. And because of that, they get more of the positions.

There's a Berkeley study that shows that men apply for the promotion when they meet 60% of the qualifications of the job. And women? They typically apply for that same promotion only when they meet 100% of the qualifications. That's right, my friend. Studies show that women often believe they need to meet 100% of the job qualifications in order to apply. Ladies—if that were true, men who meet 60% of the qualifications would not be getting these jobs—and they are. Stop holding yourself back!

So, here's my message to you. It's not about whether you meet 100% of the qualifications when applying; it's about figuring out how to do the job once you have it. Women are innately creative and resourceful. We've already established that you are a pro at delivering. You can figure it out. Apply! The world needs your strengths right now.

My mission is to see more women leading our corporations, our governments, and our communities. I'm not advocating for any women. I'm advocating for honest, service-minded women.

Remember those stats from the introduction. We are 50% of the population, 57% of college graduates, and yet we are only 8% of fortune 500 CEOs, 30% of government executives and only 2.7% beneficiaries of venture capital.

This is unacceptable.

The reason we are not at the top is NOT because we aren't smart enough.

We have to put ourselves out there and utilize our innate strengths strategically, to claim our place in leadership; not just to reach our goals but to make the world a better place. We have to use our innate strengths strategically to grow our influence, leverage our relationships, and deliver what the world needs and claim our equal place in leadership.

When you look at the polarization in our communities and among people, when you observe the ethics problems in our politics and corporations—it's the female strengths that are often missing.

I'm not saying women are better than men. As I said in the introduction, I believe that we all need both male and female strengths to succeed. When you look at some of the most respected and impactful male leaders in history, many of them utilize these same 5 female strengths to lead...people like Martin Luther King Jr., Nelson Mandela, and Mahatma Gandhi.

These leaders knew that it takes a balance to succeed. But right now, our power is out of balance. It's not about getting rid of men, it's about getting to the balance of strengths that our world needs.

It's time for another revolution lead by us. You already have what it takes, you just need to commit to going out there and utilizing your female strengths for good to build your impact, elevate your role and change the world.

Thank you for your kind attention to what is written in this book. I wish you all the success that you want and crave. I'm here for you and will support you. Always feel free to reach out with questions, and to share your stories of challenges and success. I want to hear from you and can't wait to see the great things you are going to accomplish next by building your own influence and advancing your career!

Are You Ready?
Take the Next Step.

To take the next step to increase your influence through your 5 innate female strengths, join me and other career women in my Advancing Through Influence Group Coaching sessions. You'll learn how to apply your 5 innate female strengths to the people, challenges, and opportunities in your specific situation to overcome barriers and advance your career. Contact me at lacy@lacyschoen.com and I'll get back to you quickly with information about future sessions. I'd love to support you on your journey to leverage your strengths, increase your influence, and advance your career.

References

Willard F. Harley Jr., Ph.D. (1986). *His Needs Her Needs; Building a Marriage That Lasts.* Baker Publishing Group.

Tony Robbins (2016). *MONEY Mastering the Game. 7 Simple Steps to Financial Freedom.* Simon & Schuster.

McKinsey & Company (2018) "Delivering Through Diversity."

Harvard Business Review (2019) "Research. When Gender Diversity Makes Firms More Productive."

Kevin O'Leary (2018) "Women-Run Businesses Make Me The Most Money. Here's Why." CNBC.COM

Census.gov

National Center for Education Statistics (2019) "Percentage of Degrees Acquired by Women."

Fortune 500 (2019). "The Fortune 500 List Has More Female CEOs Than Ever Before."

John Bonazzo. (2018) "Men Named John Outnumber All Women in Most American Industries." Observer.

Marcus Nolan, Tyler Moran & Barbara Kotschwar. (2016). "Is Gender Diversity Profitable? Evidence from A Global Survey." EY & The Peterson Institute for International Economics.

Nan S Russell (2016). "What Every Leaders Should Know About Trust and Influence." Psychology Today.

Matthew Lieberman, Ph.D. (2013) *Social: Why Our Brains Are Wired to Connect* Crown.

Frank Browning. (2015) "Survival Secrets: What Is It About Women That Makes Them More Resilient Than Men?" Cal Alumni Association, UC Berkley.

Tanvi Kheman. (2021). "Five Leadership Traits of Women." Harappa Education

Catalyst.org (2021) "Women's Earnings – The Pay Gap: Quick Take," (2021)

Tanya van Biesen. "Coronavirus Layoffs Could Erase Many of Women's Workplace Gains." (2020)

Catalyst. (2020). "Why Diversity & Inclusion Matter: Financial Performance."

Pat Heim, Ph.D., (2014). "Management 625, Invisible Rules." YouTube.

Pat Heim, Ph.D., Tammy Hughes, with Susan K. Golant (1992). *Hardball for Women: Winning at the Game of Business.* Penguin Group LLC.

Sheryl Sandberg, (2013) *Lean In: Women, Work and the Will to Lead.* Knopf.

Lacy Schoen

About the Author

Lacy Schoen is a writer, speaker, influence coach, and founder of Real Women Real Success, a company that teaches women how to break through power barriers and reach their career goals. Previously, Lacy spent thirty years in nonprofit management, twenty of them as a CEO, in the public policy and government services sectors. Lacy produced and hosted Cox Cable's Civic Connection; has won numerous awards including Senator Lou Correa's "Women Making a Difference"; and has twice been recognized as one of Orange County's "Women to Watch." She also hosts the podcast The Female Influencer, sharing insights, tips, and interviews for women who want to build their influence at work.

Lacy currently serves as a consultant and Co-Director of the Cal State Fullerton Women's Leadership Program, in the College of Business & Economics, and is on the Board of the Childhood Drowning Prevention Foundation, where she continues to apply her unique talent to grow organizations and increase their impact during challenging economic times.

Lacy has two grown children, a grown foster son, a granddaughter, and two dogs. She loves to travel, meditate, go on long walks by Lake Arrowhead, sit by her pool contemplating the good in the world, eat great food, and drink amazing wine. She lives in Norco, California with her husband, Dean Guccione, who most recently served as a Chief Officer with the City of Beverly Hills Fire Department.

Contact Lacy

Website: **Real Women Real Success**
realwomenrealsuccess.com

<u>Free Success Resources available on the</u>
<u>Real Women Real Success website:</u>

Win Your Day Get More Time
Process to dump "to-do's" off of your plate and gain more time for the important stuff

Get That Interview
How to submit a cover letter and resume that gets you the interview

Assess Your Level of Influence
A tool to determine how influential you are at work

The Female Influencer – *Podcast*
A bi-weekly podcast focused on strategies, tips, and interviews to help women increase their influence

<u>Success Escalators available through</u>
<u>Real Women Real Success website:</u>

Advancing Through Influence: Using Your Innate Female Strengths to Break Through Power Barriers and Advance Your Career – Book (Available on Amazon.com or at realwomenrealsuccess.com)

A book written by Lacy Schoen specifically designed to teach women how they can empower themselves by building their influence in a way that enables them to advance their career.

Keys to Conscious Business Growth – Amazon Best Seller (Available on Amazon.com or at realwomenrealsuccess.com) *A book written by 20 women for you; these often raw and honest stories of challenge and success will inspire working women*

One-on-one coaching with Lacy (Details and rates available at: realwomenrealsuccess.com)

Group coaching with Lacy and a group of your peers (Group coaching programs run several times a year. For more information go to: realwomenrealsuccess.com)

Social Media

YouTube: youtube.com/c/RealWomenRealSuccess-LacySchoen

Facebook: facebook.com/realwomenrealsuccess

Instagram: instagram.com/lacyschoen/

LinkedIn: linkedin.com/in/realwomenrealsuccesslacyschoen

Speaking Engagements:

To explore having Lacy Schoen speak at your event, please reach out to us directly at lacy@lacyschoen.com

Contact information:

Lacy Schoen
lacy@lacyschoen.com
realwomenrealsuccess.com

CPSIA information can be obtained
at www.ICGtesting.com
Printed in the USA
FSHW020857090721
82974FS

9 781735 657943